EXHAUSTED RAPUNZEL

Tales of Modern Castle Life

附 附

EXHAUSTED RAPUNZEL

Tales of Modern Castle Life

DEIRDRE REILLY

CR

Opine Publishing

Columbia, Maryland

Opine Publishing
P O Box 1239
(5113 W. Running Brook Road)
Columbia, Maryland (MD) 21044 USA
http://opinepublishing.com

Printed in the United States of America
Cover design by Robert Howard
Front cover illustration by Chris Wold Dyrud

Library of Congress Cataloging-in-Publication Data

Reilly, Deirdre.
    Exhausted Rapunzel : tales of modern castle life /
Deirdre Reilly.
    p. cm.
    ISBN 0-9708451-3-8

    1. Family — United States — Humor. 2. Marriage — United
States — Humor. 3. American wit and humor. I. Title.

PN6231.F3R45 2002   818'.602
                        QBI02-200249

Enter Deirdre Reilly's Castle –
Chances Are You'll Feel Right At Home . . .

Enter these pages and follow along as newspaper columnist Deirdre Reilly raises her family and observes the world around her in her own indelible style.

A collection of columns written over three years, **Exhausted Rapunzel—Tales of Modern Castle Life** examines the fairy tale in all of us, and takes the reader on a funny, revealing journey straight to the heart of family life.

Deirdre on Learning the Rules of Football . . .
"Mom, are you concentrating?" our ten-year-old asked me. "You look like you look when the oil man describes how our furnace works."

Deirdre on Dieting . . .
By the end of the second week I am bargaining with the kids for a Cheeto, and I find myself crooning softly with delight when I find an old M&M in the bottom of my purse.

Deirdre on Napping . . .
The Denial Napper will answer the phone with a voice that sounds like they swallowed ten thousand nails, and yet tell you that before you called they had just finished sorting their Tupperware by size and color.

Deirdre on Being Parents Again (and being a little older this time around) . . .
"Now, who planted shrubs in the middle of the

street?" I asked my husband irritably one evening, standing on the porch and burping the baby. "Those are our kids, honey," my husband answered, quickly taking the baby. "I'll get your glasses."

Deirdre on the Secret of Life . . .

I awoke with a start, and looked around. Happily-ever-after is now.

ଔ   ଔ

Contents ๛

THIS BOOK IS FOR MY HUSBAND FRED

WITH ALL MY LOVE

AND

FOR THE DADS AND MOMS IN THE ARMED FORCES

SERVING OUR COUNTRY OVERSEAS

Acknowledgements

I would like to express my thanks to a few people in particular whose help was instrumental in the making of this book.

A loving thank you to Jean Purcell, publisher of Opine Publishing, for her talent, creativity and, most especially, her vision. She put many deserving projects on hold to guide this manuscript, and I'm forever grateful.

Thanks also go to Carri Hesson for all her many and varied efforts on my behalf.

Thanks to Larry Walsh, former editor of the *Reading Advocate*, for starting my humor column and for letting it take root in our community.

A big thanks to Richard Thompson, editor of the *Wilmington Advocate* and *Tewksbury Advocate*, for keeping the column going and helping it to grow.

Thanks always to Carole.

1 ∞∞

FAMILY TOGETHERNESS OR . . . CAN I GO NOW?

"Sometimes it's the imperfections that make something beautiful. Sometimes it's better to leave well enough alone. Just ask my cat."

∞

BAD JUNK

ONCE OR TWICE a year our town makes available a "large rubbish pick-up," which is when the big trash trucks come around and take all of your unwanted items away for free if you stack them at the curb.

Now, this is a time of great rejoicing for my husband, who looked over his coffee cup at me recently and mused, "We can't miss this trash pick-up thing this year. I'll come home early the night before the trucks come and we'll empty out the garage—it should only take 20 minutes or so."

I stared at him. "Twenty minutes? Are we talking

about that garage right outside that has no room for a car? The garage that has two couches and a stove in it—the garage that, if our junk was any good, we could rent out as a furnished apartment?"

"That's the one," he answered confidently. "Now, let's circle that date on the calendar."

Three weeks later I was driving through my neighborhood and began to feel uneasy—why was everyone in the neighborhood moving? People were swarming across their front yards loaded down with old lamps, broken tables and the like. And then it hit me. "Large rubbish removal!" I yelled, turning the car around. "We've got to get home, kids!"

Thirty minutes later my husband screeched up to the curb, flinging himself out of the car and in the direction of the garage. "How did we forget that tomorrow is pickup day?" he panted, hoisting a small canoe onto his shoulders and, unbuttoning his suit coat and flipping his tie over his shoulder, lugging the canoe down to the curb. Squirrels began bailing out of the canoe at a furious pace, flying through the air and into nearby trees until it looked like the "flying monkeys" scene from *The Wizard of Oz*. Our kids looked on, vastly amused.

We agreed on the first few items we put at the curb—two couches, a fake plastic tree and an old broken stereo system. Throw in a Duran Duran poster and a beer mug collection and you have our very first apartment after we were married resurrected there on the curb.

It was the next few items we started to argue over—it turns out I'm a "keeper" and my husband's a "discarder." I see possible uses for everything and hence was heard to say some of the following sentences:

- "You don't know for certain I'll never teach badminton lessons."

- "Oh, goody! I've been looking for this life raft!"
- "Remember when I was going to make a fortune selling papier-mâché doorknob covers? Here they are!"

I stopped my husband from putting three rusty old scooters in the discard pile, telling him I thought that one day we could build a room onto the back of the house and hang the scooters from the walls—kind of a "theme" room.

He answered, "Not unless you're planning on opening a restaurant in the back of the house."

He also found a box of rocks in the garage—plain old garden-variety rocks. "Uh, honey?" he grunted, shoving the box of rocks down the driveway with his foot while balancing an old dented bed frame across his shoulders.

"Oh, don't go anywhere with those rocks," I said, bustling over importantly. "Those are for the goldfish pond I'm going to build in the backyard. I found an article in the paper that tells you exactly how to do it."

"A goldfish pond!" he yelled in exasperation. "We can't even fit two lawn chairs back there it's so overgrown—but you're building a goldfish pond? And I thought we decided, no more pets!"

Gradually the pile on the curb grew, until it dwarfed all the other piles in the neighborhood. I kept sneaking things out of the pile so that basically my husband was walking down the driveway with one item while I was circling around the side of the house with another item.

Finally we were done. We noticed that pick-up trucks and vans were circling around the neighborhood—these smaller vehicles were checking out junk and taking whatever they liked for their own uses. The vehicles would come up to look at our impressive pile, but no one wanted our junk and, perversely, we were hurt.

"What's wrong with our junk?" I wondered aloud, dusting off some plastic fruit and propping it inside a rusty old ice skate. "Maybe if I put the plastic palm tree next to the ripped beanbag chairs, that will bring 'em in."

"We have bad junk," my husband said reflectively, watching other piles being picked through.

"That's just the way it goes sometimes," I sighed.

I made sure not to be home the next day when the big trucks came—I don't necessarily want to be associated with bad junk. I'm working on it, though. I went right out to the store, pledging to myself—from now on I'm buying only top-quality junk, and that's just the way it is.

❧

LEARNING FOOTBALL

THERE ARE MANY reasons why I love my friend Pam, a dear friend from Connecticut. She's sweet, she's funny and, maybe most impressive of all, she likes football. Pam even *understands* football. As close as she and I are, this is where we part ways.

It is now football season—or as I like to call it, The Season Of My Great Aloneness. My husband is a big football fan, so we go from real conversation all summer long to grunts and hand signals in the fall. I don't really invest the time in understanding too many of the professional sporting events—I recently said to my husband, "So when is March Madness?" You see what I mean.

This year, like every other year, I plan to sit down for two seconds and learn about football. Like, the rules—so that this will be something my husband and I can share together. (Having three kids, four pets and an overwhelming mortgage just isn't enough.) Each year when I repeat this intention aloud, my husband must know how Charlie Brown feels when Lucy promises to hold the football for him so that he can kick it—he knows the results will be disastrous, but he's gonna try anyway.

I remember last year's attempt. "Now," my husband started out, throwing a few crackers into his mouth, "you have to understand that football is a game of downs." I sat at attention on our family room couch, posture erect, head inclined towards him, displaying a complete absorption in our topic. But what I was thinking was, *The furniture in here is just all wrong. What was I thinking, ordering a chair that big?* What came out of my mouth was, "Football is a game of downs."

"Mom, are you concentrating?" our ten-year-old asked me. "You look like you look when the oil man describes how our furnace works."

"Oh, I'm listening, all right. This is going to be fun!" I arranged the crackers into a smiley-face for the boys as the announcer introduced the two teams.

My husband looked over at me doubtfully. "How about if we just watch for a few minutes and see where that takes us," he said.

The game began (I can't remember who was playing—a blue team was playing a red team). My husband and sons were totally absorbed, and I tried my best to become absorbed as well. The coach for one of the teams paced back and forth on the sidelines, barking orders into a headset.

"He looks stressed out," I said sympathetically. "Is

he a nice man? He seems like a nice man." They all looked at me as though I had five heads.

Suddenly they tensed up, craning their necks toward the screen. "Go, go, go!" they yelled.

"Yeah, go," I echoed, trying to figure out where exactly the ball was. While many players rushed for yardage (translation: *as the game droned on*), I was developing a list of questions for half time: 1. Why were the players so rough? 2. Why was a dishtowel tucked into the quarterback's pants? 3. Why can't they ban professional cheerleaders from the face of the earth?

The phone rang in the other room and my older son answered it, coming back into the TV room and saying, "Mom, it's for you. I think it's a telemarketer."

"I'd better get that—it might be important," I said, jumping up and running into the other room.

"I'm sensing your level of interest in the game is waning!" my husband shouted after me.

Fifteen minutes later, after the telemarketer tearfully said, "Please, ma'am, I just don't know any more about replacement windows—can't I have a representative call you back?" I headed back into the TV room.

"Come watch this, honey," my husband said, motioning to the screen. I watched as a player dragged himself, the ball, and about 20 guys who were on top of him across one of the white lines on the field. "Now, what has he accomplished?" my husband asked me.

"Um, a first down," I answered. (Shot in the dark.) The boys looked impressed, my husband laughed, and I gave a look of being just overwhelmed by so much learning.

I gradually eased out of the room and reflected on how true it is that we learn what we're interested in. My husband knows the rules of every sport on the planet, my kids have memorized our video store account number, and I have almost perfected a contraption that flips chocolate chip cookies into my mouth while I'm reading.

I laughed in wonder at how amazing we humans are, and went to call Pam. Of course, she couldn't talk just then—she was watching the game. Great gal.

ভ

THE SCIENCE PROJECT THAT FELL TO EARTH

THERE IS A word in the English language that strikes fear and terror in every parent's heart. That word is not "measles," nor is it "college" or "cavity." That word, my friends, is "posterboard."

When a parent hears the word "posterboard," he or she knows that a project is due soon from their school-age child and that the project is going to involve some creative artwork. Parents feel, perhaps unreasonably, that they themselves are going to be judged by the quality of the finished project, and that can bring out old fears and feelings of inadequacy.

As a child, I was never talented at the creative arts—my clay ashtray made my parents quit smoking. My woven potholders contained asbestos and involved a trip to the hospital. I was sent to the principal's office for a "talk with the nice man" after I finished a noodle art project in kindergarten.

So I get downright grumpy when a project involving creative artwork is due from one of my kids. Now, I shouldn't feel this way, mainly because it is my child's project and not mine; and it's my child's creativity, and not mine, being evaluated. But let's face it, the heat is on.

Some parents become what you might call "overly involved" in these projects: when a kid's mock-up of the Solar System involves a laser light show, fiber-optic cables and an actual trip into Outer Space, chances are there's a parent waiting in the wings somewhere.

At the other end of the spectrum, there are those parents who choose to stay completely uninvolved at project time, giving the kid a hearty clap on the back and a "let me know how it all turns out" upon hearing of a project. These are also the parents who will suggest syrup as a handy alternative to glue when no actual glue can be found.

I guess I'm somewhere in the middle of these two groups.

Our last project started something like this: my ten-year-old son and I were driving along after a satisfactory trip to our local drug store—a trip in which he had obtained a ten-pound bag of candy corn, and I obtained $1,000 worth of cosmetics that I could fit into my wallet.

We were cruising along in companionable silence, and I remember that I was planning out the rest of my evening: I was going to 1) try on new cosmetics, 2) get into pajamas and have a cup of tea, and 3) get in bed and watch *I Love Lucy* while drinking tea.

Suddenly, my son jumped in his seat and muttered, "Oh my gosh."

"What is it, honey?" I asked, still happily planning my evening.

"Oh, nothing," he answered. "I just remembered

something."

Now, I'm a parent, so I know all the warning signs, and all the warning signs were there: it was a school night, kids can be forgetful, and the evening was just going too darn well. My whole system was on red alert.

"What did you remember?" I asked casually, while my insides were screaming, *"Danger, Will Robinson! Danger!"*

"Ummm, I have a little project due tomorrow—just a little one. I just remembered I have to go home and build an alien for science class. I may need some posterboard."

There was that dreaded word. Minutes later my son and I dashed into the house where my husband was sprawled out on the couch innocently reading the paper.

"Get up and start searching for materials that we can use to build an alien!" I shouted, frantically casting my eyes around the room. "Do we have posterboard?" My husband jumped up.

"What are our parameters?" he immediately asked. "How long have we had to do the assignment, and when is it due?"

"Tomorrow," my son and I answered, searching kitchen cabinets for materials. We came up with an egg carton, two sandwich baggies, some potato chips (I was hungry) and some magic markers. We got to work, as my beautiful evening evaporated in front of my eyes.

"I wanted to give him some antennae," my son mumbled, looking to no avail in our junk drawer.

"Snip some hair off of the cat," my husband said, as the cat walked through the room.

Luckily, my son chose to use some old, bald pipe cleaners I can't even remember buying (I think they came with the house).

Suddenly, without realizing it, I was engrossed in the project. All my past art class failures were forgotten—it was a brave new day.

"Maybe we could give him a little smile, you know, like he's happy to be on our planet," I mused, drawing out some preliminary sketches on a paper towel. "Honey," I asked my husband, "where is the drill?"

My son and my husband exchanged glances.

"Mom, it's my project," my son reminded me, coloring the egg carton with the magic markers.

"Oh, I know, sweetheart," I chuckled, carefully gluing things to other things. "By the way, what is our alien's motivation? Why is he here on Earth?"

While I was waiting for the answer my husband suggested that maybe our son should finish up alone.

Later that evening I snuck downstairs to look at the project as it stood drying on a square of paper towels on the kitchen table. I knew that we would be carefully transporting this alien to school in the morning, and I knew that the alien was perfect just as he was, with no grown-up embellishments. (And we didn't even need posterboard.)

Sometimes it's the imperfections that make something beautiful. Sometimes it's better to leave well enough alone. Just ask my cat.

CR

HOME SICK

THREE OUT OF five people in my family caught a bad flu bug that was going around recently, and we were not a pretty sight for about a week or so. The whole family dynamic changes when there's an illness in the house—the people who are sick just hang on for dear life as one day melts into another, while the people who are well go about their business and basically represent the family out there in the world.

I was the first to come down with this particular flu.

"So, are you going to be all right?" my husband asked, looking down at me as I lay huddled on the bathroom floor wrapped in an afghan and trying to remember all the names of the Seven Dwarfs (I think I had a fever). "You know I have that meeting today," he said apologetically, stepping over me to straighten his tie in the mirror.

"Oh, sure," I moaned, as I tried to lick the last of the medicine out of an old, expired bottle of cough syrup, "don't let a little thing like my death stop you. Have a good day, now."

"Well, okay, if you say so," he said, closing the door quickly behind him.

"Get some ginger ale on the way home!" I yelled after him, the sentence he would hear every day for a week.

Next my kids came home, one by one, sick with the same flu bug.

"Dropping off or picking up?" the school secretary would say sympathetically as I dragged myself into the school to sign out one boy or another for the day.

"Picking up," I would say, looking very stylish in

my old sweats, uncombed hair (Bed Head) and lipstick that looked like it was drawn on by a distracted pre-schooler.

On one visit I was approached by a "together" mom—the woman in the neighborhood whose jeans are creased, her kids get straight A's, her lawn never turns brown and her car never breaks down.

"How are you?" she asked, watching the baby pull lint balls off my sweatshirt and then try to feed them to me. "We're never sick at our house," she laughed. "It must be all the home-grown herbs we eat."

I explained that I've been trying to grow some Tylenol and Excedrin shrubs in our backyard, but I plant the capsules and nothing ever happens.

The kids and I were shut in together for several days and together we learned many things, including:

1. Home Depot sells a special pair of pliers that can open child-proof medicine bottles;
2. thoroughly-jelled Jell-O is nice, but you can also drink it if it's taking too long;
3. sticking a thermometer in your child's armpit is useless if he's ticklish.

The kids also learned something about me while we were all home sick together—I'm a closet soap opera watcher. I've tried to hide it, but since I've been at home with our third baby, I'm hooked on one of these programs again.

They found out like this: we were all huddled under our blankets throwing a box of tissues back and forth to each other and watching TV. Suddenly, the theme music for my favorite soap, *The Edge Of My Madness*, came on. I perked up.

"Mom, you don't watch this, do you?" the kids snuffled, smirking.

"Of course not," I snuffled back, my eyes secretly riveted to the screen. "These programs are ridiculous—don't touch that remote."

So we watched while characters with names like Drake and Stormy said sentences like, "I had a lot of time to think while I was trapped in the aqueduct," and "I learned a lot about myself when I was caught switching the lab results during that ice storm."

Darned if after a while the kids weren't interested too—"Mom, do you think that Tad and Dixie's love will last?" my ten-year-old asked groggily as he was falling asleep later that day.

"At least till next week," I assured him gently, tucking his covers in around him. The program put our own troubles into perspective.

"Things could be worse, always remember that," was my motherly advice to my children the next afternoon, pointing to the TV screen. "You could be like Dirk Kinkle there, looking at five to ten in Statesville Prison for running an underground scam operation while pretending to be a nuclear physicist, which was hard, what with his multiple personalities and all." I think they got my point.

So, my husband was stuck with the job of running the household every evening as soon as he got home from work so that I could rest.

Things started to slide downhill—the baby was wearing a diaper and a turtleneck to bed at night, and one evening at dinner I heard everyone laughing over a hearty dinner of Cocoa Puffs and orange soda.

The house developed a thin layer of dust over everything, and the plastic plants died.

Soon my husband was in bed with the same flu, trying to remember the names of the Seven Dwarfs and begging for ginger ale.

"Don't worry about your dad," I winked at the kids as they left for school for the day. "Today your father is going to watch a little TV with me."

Funny, but my husband got better and was back to work in record time.

Ꮗ

VINCENT & ME

AT LEAST ONCE or twice in every child's life, a good parent makes sure that said child visits an art gallery. Now, children will stare at television, they will stare at video games, they will even stare at their mother while she is flossing her teeth. For some reason, though, through the centuries children have had trouble staring at art.

This opportunity came for my oldest two children, ages 11 and 14, on a recent sunny weekend when the rest of the planet went away to the beach or to some other fun locale. I proposed that we go downtown, look at some art, and improve ourselves!

My husband was not completely thrilled. I knew this because he suddenly became very interested in re-paving the driveway and felt a deep and abiding concern for the washing machine, which for the better part of two years had been spewing out water and detergent during the spin cycle. I ignored this. A little art would be good for him, too. Plus, he owed me. I had watched golf on TV with him the weekend before and still hadn't gotten over it. So, over the shrieks of protest (his), we made our plans.

For some reason, children like to try and bargain

in these situations, and they always use fast food to do it.

"We'll go to the stupid old museum or whatever if you get us Burger King," they whined.

"This is not a bargaining situation," I said, knowing darn well we'd be coming home with Whoppers and fries. "Consider yourselves lucky; while your friends are diving into the same old boring waves at the beach and driving the same old boring go-carts and visiting the same old arcades, you'll be using art to find out more about yourselves! Now, let's hustle!"

So, off we went down the highway, passing carload after carload of children who were actually happy. I, meanwhile, was feeling very serious. We were going to become a more serious family in general; we would attend the opera, perhaps learn to speak Latin, whatever. Gone were the days where my kids pronounced Chopin as "choppin" and meant it. Goodbye to times when Michelangelo was only a warrior turtle. Just as I was contemplating what sort of hairdo would go with my new serious self, we approached the art gallery.

As we walked through the front doors of the Museum of Fine Arts in Boston, I felt it would behoove the kids to go in with a little background knowledge.

"There are many different styles of art that have been created in several different time zones," I explained. "Take, for example, artists known as *Impressionists*."

I leaned in to whisper my knowledge as we stood in line for tickets. "These artists wanted to make a good impression on people, hence the name, 'Impressionist'." I winked knowingly. "I believe there were some self-esteem issues with these artists, if you know what I mean."

I must have been on to something. Others in line were actually listening with a look of disbelief on their faces.

We were lucky enough to be at the art gallery on a day when a Van Gogh exhibit was also there (we naturally pretended to our kids that we knew all along we were coming to see Van Gogh).

Of course, this exhibit was sold out, so we stood to the side of the exit door and heard people mutter things like "I am completely changed as a person" and "I will view everything and everyone differently from now on." So we didn't miss much.

Touring through the different rooms of art I came up with a few different handy rules for art viewing.

1. Clasp your hands behind your back when looking at a painting, then scrunch your face up and walk around it looking puzzled.
2. Say the phrase "I'm a fan of his earlier works" as often as possible.
3. Do not sit down to rest on anything that has a descriptive plaque on it; they yell at you for this.
4. Egyptian caskets do not double as diaper changing tables.
5. The dark rooms are scary.

After about an hour and a half, the baby was ready to go. We could tell because he was making his own art all over his face with an old Milk Dud he found in his stroller.

I was pleased that my teen-ager in particular seemed to be absorbing all that I was saying until I realized that he had had earphones on the whole time.

As we walked out (actually it was more like jogging trying to keep up with my husband), I felt as if we were leaving Vincent Van Gogh behind, as if he were wondering why we hadn't looked at his paintings.

"We'll be back," I said to a poster of his face hanging above us from the ceiling.

Outside, an old woman kissed her husband on the cheek, leaving a mark of pink on his wrinkled skin as they headed for a seat on a bench. That was art. I think Vincent would have thought so, too.

෴

BOSSY BACKPACKS

I MUST HAVE had a very strange dream recently. At least that's what I'm telling myself—that's the only way to explain the stunning events that occurred one night when I crept downstairs to get a drink of water.

As I was standing at the sink, I heard a "Psst! Over here, lady!" I wheeled around, but nothing seemed amiss—all was still and peaceful in the kitchen.

I shrugged and turned to leave the kitchen when again I heard, "I say, look over this way!"

Following the sound, I cautiously walked over to a coat rack where my kids hang their backpacks after school.

"That's better—step right on over here!" To my amazement, the sound was coming from my ten-year-old's backpack. I rubbed my forehead, confused.

"You can't be talking . . . you're a backpack!" I mumbled, stepping back.

"And you're a grownup, which doesn't stop you from eating every piece of Halloween candy you've bought well before Halloween," the backpack said. "You think your family doesn't notice the chocolate smudges on your face? They're just being nice."

I looked at this somewhat rude mass of nylon and

zippers. "Listen, I bought you, I can make sure you tote nothing but encyclopedias from here on out, pal."

"Point taken," the backpack said agreeably. "I just thought maybe we should have a talk about some of the things going on around here."

"Like what?" I asked.

"Well, for starters, what's the deal with the snacks I carry to school for my young friend? I realize that sometimes you just can't make it to the store, but white bread with syrup smeared on it and a thermos full of Sanka just doesn't cut it," he said. "And what about the time you sent him with a glass of orange juice propped up in his snack bag, telling him to take the most level way to school possible? Get to the store and buy some juice boxes, woman! It's appalling."

"Okay, okay," I muttered, "I hear you. But since you know so much, you know how I send him with nutritious snacks nine times out of ten."

"And I've still got most of them right here!" the backpack screeched. "Don't you ever clean me out? I'm currently carrying two moldy Pop-Tarts, a PTA notice from last month, a rotten banana, a field trip notice that was due last Monday, and ten rocks of various sizes and weights. It's not easy, I tell you!" He swayed back and forth, which I thought was a bit dramatic.

"Anything else?" I sighed.

"Since you mention it," he sniffed, "how about making sure that I make it home on the weekends? Last weekend I spent two whole days at the bottom of your neighbor's car, buried under soccer balls and hockey sticks until suddenly I became the most important thing on the planet on Sunday night at about 8:30. There I was, carrying important homework and school notices, and our young friend had completely forgotten me! It makes a backpack want to weep."

"Hey, listen, we do our best," I said consolingly. "We like to think that we're sensitive, intelligent people."

"Intelligent!" he snorted. "Have you ever listened to yourselves helping with homework? It's pathetic. I hate to be the one to tell you, but the Louisiana Purchase had nothing to do with a new Macy's, Karl Marx did not have a brother named Zeppo, and believe it or not, photosynthesis occurs even when you don't have a camera!"

"Say, now, enough's enough," I said, defensively. "I may just toss you right down into the basement."

"The old backpack graveyard," the backpack said sadly. "You've never bothered to replace the old furnace, but you've spent a total of five thousand dollars on backpacks for the kids. You could move everything you own out of this house in backpacks."

"Hey, zip it," I retorted.

"Oh, goody, backpack humor," the backpack said. "Listen, before you go could you talk to the toaster? He's a little depressed—the smoke alarm keeps scaring him."

The next morning I came downstairs warily, glancing at the backpacks hanging quietly in the corner.

"So, has anyone seen or heard anything unusual around here this morning?" I inquired casually to my family, to be met with stares and shrugs.

After everyone left for work and school I listened appreciatively to the silence all around me.

"Well, whatever that was last night, it sure was weird," I said to myself.

The dog, lying at my feet, rolled over and stretched. "You can say that again," she yawned.

CR

A COWGIRL IN OUR MIDST

THERE AREN'T A lot of cowgirls around anymore. By *cowgirls* I mean women who can tame the land, cook you a gourmet meal out of a potato and a pot of water, wrassle wild animals, and rock babies to sleep. Luckily, I have one of the few remaining cowgirls left, right here in my own family; her name is Mary Helen, and she's my grandma.

Mary Helen was born in Beech Grove, Tennessee, and was married by the time she was 14—not unusual in her part of the country and back in those days. In my own girlhood I was amazed by this and questioned my grandmother with all the inquisitiveness and sensitivity my liberal arts public school education could muster.

"Grammy," I began (I remember we were sitting in a car outside the 7-11 and my mother had run in to get bread), "what was the hardest thing, emotionally and mentally, of course, about marrying at that age— barely a young woman?"

Mary Helen considered this question seriously for a moment, then answered, "I had to get rid of my horse and my gun." That's what she said.

Mary Helen's true love was the young man she married way back when, and she had three babies with him—she gave birth to my dad at home in her bed, the doctor too far away to call.

"Grammy," I said, amazed at this, "what was the thing you remember most—physically and mentally, of course—about having dad at home?"

Mary Helen considered this for a moment (I remember she was standing at the stove) and answered, "I was sure glad when it was over."

Mary Helen is a gifted artist. One painting she did, of two Native American men gliding through the Florida Everglades in a canoe while surrounded by crocodiles, has always symbolized to me Mary Helen's imagination and creativity. She says, "That one used up a lot of green paint."

Mary Helen just told me recently that she had a nephew named Paul who died at the young age of two, during the Depression. Paul had been living with his grandparents—Mary Helen's parents—when his own parents took him away, desperately believing that they could survive and care for their baby on their own. Paul died of starvation. This was the first time I had ever heard of Paul.

"Grammy," I said over the phone line, "how did any of you get over losing Paul?"

There was a weighty silence on the other end of the line. "Momma and Daddy begged them not to take that baby away till times were easier," was Mary Helen's quiet reply.

Mary Helen loves a good laugh; once, upon returning to the cemetery where her husband lay buried, she noticed that the grave site and double headstone created for her and her husband were unequal; my grandfather's side was weeded and trimmed and polished, while her side—dates not yet carved in—was overgrown and in pretty sore shape. She turned to the minister of the church, who happened to be with her on her visit, and said, "My side looks kind of neglected, don't you think?"

The minister mopped his brow and answered, "Mary Helen, you're not using it yet!" She loved that.

In the last few years Mary Helen has moved away

from her home and her home state, and she has lost her sight. She just keeps right on going.

On a recent vacation at the beach, I pulled salt water taffy from my teeth while I watched Mary Helen crochet five or six dishwashing cloths, sew a button on one of my kids' shorts, and feel her way all around the unfamiliar rental house, memorizing it in no time.

Some day, I thought, I will have grandkids who will ask me about her. I could tell them the funny stories or show them her artwork, but I think instead I will try to explain the way Mary Helen looks when grace is being said at the supper table. Her long body kind of folds in on itself, and her proud gray head drops in worship, in obedience, in tune. She goes where sometimes she talks and sometimes she listens; she goes where Paul is being fed.

My prayers, sitting shoulder to shoulder with her, are different. "Lord," I ask, "let us keep her."

After all, there aren't too many cowgirls left.

CR

2 ॡॡ

ACTUALIZING MY LITTLE OL' SELF

---

*". . . one article advised brushing my eyebrows up
and out with a toothbrush for a full, yet defined
look. They should have mentioned that you should
use a new toothbrush; I went out to lunch one day
with toothpaste stuck in my eyebrows."*

ॡ

THE DROOL FACTOR

B EING A STAY-AT-HOME mom has been a worth-
while choice for me and one I have been fortunate
enough to be able to make. In addition to being able to
witness every part of my kids' development, being at
home has allowed me to express myself creatively and
to practice, and become consistently better at, something I consider an art form: the afternoon nap.

I was napping way before napping was "in" and
"cool." When the Surgeon General announced that
napping was healthy and recommended it every day

for everyone, I turned to my family with tear-filled eyes and whispered gratefully, "I knew it! Vindicated at last!"

I personally have always thought that I should live my life somewhere like Mexico where the whole country naps due to the heat and it is an accepted part of the culture. Unfortunately, my husband doesn't feel that the availability of siestas is a good enough reason to move.

Sadly for me, my family wakes up chipper, bops through their day chipper, and practically has to be knocked out to go to sleep at night; so a Napper in their midst is looked at with patient indulgence.

Nappers are usually in one of two categories—those who admit the nap and those who do not. You can call an Admitted Napper at two in the afternoon, and when you ask if you have woken them up, they will cheerfully and groggily tell you that yes, they were asleep.

A Denial Napper will answer the phone with a voice that sounds like they swallowed ten thousand nails, and yet tell you that before you called they had just finished sorting their Tupperware by size and color. If in a very deep sleep, the confused Denial Napper may answer the phone using the name of their place of business—you may hear a breathless "Bertucci's—Brick Oven Pizza." Don't order anything; it will never show up.

I myself am a Denial Napper, unless I answer the phone and no actual sound comes out of my mouth— the dreaded voice-robbing nap. After squeaking out a few mouse-like sounds, the phone is put down while the throat is violently cleared.

A Denial Napper will visit at their front door very cheerily, even animatedly, when interrupted by a visitor. I myself have stood talking for long periods of time only to realize when I shut the door that my clothes are a twisted wreck and that my face looks like a roadmap, crisscrossed with sleep lines. I always wonder if the visitor took my wise comments on health care reform seriously after that.

My family knows the warning signs of an impending nap—a yawn, the glazed eyes, and a casual "I think I'll go upstairs and see what's on Lifetime Television for Women." Any movie entitled something like "Moment of Truth—A Mother's Deception" is a good breeding ground for a nap.

Some people will tell you they can't nap, either due to superior genetics or the fact that if they lie down they're gone for the day.

Others will tell you that all they need is a good 20 minutes, and they are completely recharged. Twenty minutes is not a nap; some commercials are longer. I say to these people, "Don't give up!" Napping takes practice.

True napping has to involve being two things: unconscious and willing to put off work you know you should be doing. These are also the same requirements that apply to some elected officials.

Napping can also be some creative downtime; I have resolved many issues while napping. Through dreams I have personally solved the national debt, rewired the air traffic pattern over Logan Airport, and found the Dream Barbie I lost in second grade.

There is one sticky issue to napping, especially if it is done in public: the drool factor.

Being an exhausted mom, I often catch a few winks when traveling. There is just no experience like waking up in the middle of an airplane trip only to realize that your mouth has been hanging open while pointed in the direction of a fellow passenger who, to avoid you, has been trying to climb out onto the wing of the plane.

There is also nothing like waking up suddenly during a car ride to find your loved one gently wiping your mouth with napkins because you have been steadily drooling on yourself.

Why do you think babies live in bibs? Sometimes modern life is just one big search for sleep.

So, when encountering Nappers, be kind. Treat them with patience, with respect, and above all, don't wake them up.

They're so cute when they're asleep.

CR

DIET TIPS

I HAVE JUST started a diet. I'm really going to lose those pesky ten pounds, I tell myself, with a sensible diet and the addition of daily exercise (unfortunately my doctor doesn't consider straightening up the family room forty times a day to be true exercise).

I usually feel the need to shed a few unwanted pounds most intensely at the beginning of summer, when I lug everyone's summer clothes down from the attic.

As I open up the box labeled "Mom's Clothes" and pull out a pair of shorts, I frown, puzzled. Holding the shorts out in front of me I think to myself, *There's been some mistake! The boys' clothes must have gotten in my box!*

I pull out tank tops that look like washcloths, little summer dresses that must have "shrunk in the wash," and, worst of all, bathing suits that look so small all I can do is sit and have one of those long, cleansing, hysterical laughing fits.

I immediately re-group. I can just wear tee shirts all summer, along with baggy shorts; I'll get kind of a relaxed, beachy look going for myself. Or I could wear some of my husband's smaller clothes! Or maybe it won't get that hot this summer and I can just keep wearing sweatshirts!

But then a better, stronger part of myself takes over and I think, *No, I can do this! I'll just lose a few pounds; it should take, oh, about a week!* And so it begins.

I always start the diet with the exercise part. The best part of exercising is buying the clothes. (My current sneakers, which are used for everything but exercise, were purchased at Caldor's in 1988 for $12.99, and are so old they light up in the back when I walk.)

So, recently I went and bought some fancy new sneakers, some new workout outfits, and I was all set. I felt lighter just driving home from the mall.

Okay, I told myself. *I'm going to walk for one hour each day. No. I will walk for one hour each day, plus walk to do all my errands. In fact,* I told myself, getting carried away, *I will not even use the car anymore, except for special occasions. Maybe I'll run the next Boston Marathon,* I mused! (I was not yet actually walking when I thought all this—I was still on my porch in my new clothes, perusing my mail.)

An hour later, as I was straggling up a hill gasping for air carrying two grocery sacks that weighed as much as cannonballs, I re-thought my exercise plan. I dropped to the ground when I reached home, and my diet food sprawled all over the lawn. I blew a kiss to my car.

The first couple of days of a diet I am on a "diet high," guzzling down water every couple of hours until I gurgle more than I speak, eating my fruit, and generally feeling pretty proud of my shrinking self.

My husband usually joins me in these diets, although he just adds an apple and a banana to his regular meals. I guess he feels that the apple and banana counteract the pizza, burgers, and anything else he can slap cheese on that he eats throughout the week.

We start eating foods that have uplifting, congratulatory names: SnackWell's, Sweet Rewards, Smart Ones. One night I overheard my husband telling the kids that they had better go get a new attitude and I bolted down the stairs, thinking that he was directing them to a new brand of diet dessert.

Some of these foods are actually pretty good; my nine-year-old and I were wrestling over the last row of SnackWell's Devil's Food cookies by day four of the diet.

By the end of the second week I am bargaining with the kids for a Cheeto, and I find myself crooning softly with delight when I find an old M&M in the bottom of my purse.

My new sneakers seem to be logging more hours under the bed than on the open road, and I am sick of putting my Lean Cuisine dinners on a coffee cup saucer to make them appear bigger.

So, to end the diet I simply say to my husband, "Do you think I need to lose weight?" The man is a deer caught in the headlights. Being no fool, he tells me that of course I don't need to lose weight; I'm perfect the way I am. Ta-Dah! Diet completed.

That is, of course, until I drag the fall clothes down in a month or two. If I should mistake my favorite heavy sweater for a bedspread, I'm right back in business.

CR

FASHION PLATE

FASHION SENSE—I don't have any, and I'd like to know where to get some. I can't keep up with current fashion trends; am I supposed to look '40s, '60s, '70s, '90s or something more futuristic? Whatever the decade the exhausted look was in, that's probably where I belong.

I do make an effort when it comes to fashion, that's for sure. But my teenage son has let me know that he would prefer that I not teeter downtown in platform sneakers (kind of the way he prefers that I not drive through town obliviously belting out "Good Lovin' Gone Bad" along with the radio).

Also, the kids let me know it's probably time to pack away my favorite poncho and my leg warmers (à la *Flashdance*), so I started paying a little more attention to all things fashionable.

I found a fashion show on TV and figured I'd give it a look-see. Women who weigh as much as my whole pocketbook wandered down the runway with blank stares on their faces—amazingly enough the same exact look I get around here when I say that it's bedtime.

I learned that if I wear a Hefty bag with a nice belt (and a trashcan lid on my head), carry a parrot under one arm and smirk, I will be at the height of what's hot in Paris next fall.

Men have it much easier when it comes to fashion. Nowadays the rumpled, grungy look is in; my husband is actually at the height of fashion when he stumbles to the bathroom at 4:00 a.m. to get a drink of water, so we've decided to start going out on dates then.

I started reading a few of the prevailing fashion magazines and was immediately puzzled. I'm supposed to be able to do my make-up in the morning in seven minutes, when it takes me an hour to put my contacts in.

Under make-up tips, one article advised brushing my eyebrows up and out with a toothbrush for a full, yet defined look. They should have mentioned that you should use a new toothbrush; I went out to lunch one day with toothpaste stuck in my eyebrows.

False eyelashes are back in, but I got tired of hearing that I have "spiders under my eyes" from my nine-year-old.

Another tip was to go with a sheer, glossy lipstick this spring—I tried Vaseline as a cheap alternative but my lips got glued together and I made desperate smacking noises when I talked.

Another tip from a magazine was to look around the house for objects I could make into jewelry for a unique, "art-deco" look. I tried, but frankly my Saran Wrap necklace was too loud, and my thumbtack anklet made me cranky.

I recently asked a saleslady at a department store for help. "Are you sure about this?" I asked, slowly twirling around in front of the mirror wearing hip-hugger bellbottoms, clogs, and a smiley-face tee shirt. "I have to go to the grocery store later."

Assured that I was at the height of style, I clumped over to the make-up counter where they sprinkled me with sparkles, plucked out all my eyebrows and drew them back in again.

They then directed me to the hair salon where they put gel in my hair and flattened it to the sides of my face (I can also achieve this look by sleeping for 15 hours).

"Voilà!" the hair lady announced, and I turned to see myself. All I can say is that I looked exactly like a very worn-out, confused Ali McGraw in *Love Story*— the scene where she's dying. I decided that the retro-seventies look wasn't for me.

The '40s look is also popular, so I put dishtowels in the shoulders of some blouses and gave everyone very dramatic looks, but that wasn't me either. Some designers favor the futuristic outer-space look, but I draw the line at wearing a traffic cone on my head.

So, I'm stuck where I started, at the depths of fashion. The kids were actually somewhat relieved when I abandoned my quest for a sense of style—the only people they want money spent on for clothing is themselves. They were concerned, however, when I came through the door recently holding a shopping bag.

"Look at this!" I crowed, pulling what looked like a huge woolly mammoth out of the bag.

"What is it?" they cried, edging towards the door.

"A new poncho!" I answered, smiling sweetly.

CR

BABY NEEDS HIS COOKIES

WELL, SUMMER IS here again, and to me that means, at this moment, only one thing—it's time to diet.

When you talk to people in stilted gasps because your shorts are too tight, it's time to diet.

When your kids call you up from the basement to sit on their suitcase so that it will close, it's time to diet.

When you hiss and run from the sight of a scale the way a vampire hides from the light of day, it's time to diet.

I guess you could say that I'm using the birth of our third baby as a crutch, because I like to blame any weight gain on his arrival—but that's a step up from when I used to blame it on the birth of our second (he was ten years old at the time).

The reality is: a healthy diet takes willpower, sacrifice, and effort. Who has time for that?

Part of the problem is my actual food intake. To analyze how much I was eating every day, I made a list, similar to a menu, of what I'm actually eating all day long. Bear in mind that I have two older boys and then the baby.

BREAKFAST
2 cups TRIX cereal
14 Arrowroot baby cookies
½ jar baby bananas
1 cup coffee
1 Hi-C juice box found smashed at the bottom
    of a backpack

MORNING SNACK
14 Arrowroot baby cookies
1 glass warm tap water
25 Cheez-Its
2 cups leftover tuna casserole (unheated)

LUNCH
½ can Spaghettio's
¼ jar baby peas (licked off high chair tray)
14 Arrowroot baby cookies
1 cup cold coffee
1 corn muffin baby threw against the wall
    onto floor
I snack size bag 3-D Cool Ranch Doritos

And so on.

"I don't see any obvious trends here," I said to my husband, who was looking over my shoulder. He cleared his throat, looking like a man thinking about entering a cage with an angry, carbohydrate-addicted tiger.

"I was thinking, maybe if you didn't have so many Arrowroot cookies every day . . . just a suggestion . . . ."

"Hold on a minute!" I answered, maybe a little too quickly. "The baby loves those! Why, he wouldn't be the happy baby he is today without Arrowroot cookies! The nerve," I huffed.

"Mom, the baby hasn't seen an Arrowroot cookie in weeks," my teen-ager observed (teens are so brave). "He'd have to fight you for them." He was grounded but quick, by the way.

So, the dieting began. The first approach I took was the "starvation" approach. This is where you drink sinkfuls of water and don't eat. Now, this just doesn't work. You don't want your contribution to every conversation you're a part of to be, "I'm dizzy."

And when you fall, you fall hard; I had so many

Chips Ahoy! cookies after this approach that I just carried the bag around with me like a purse—I would just throw my keys and wallet right into the cookie bag before leaving the house.

The next approach was the "high protein" diet, espoused by many diet experts who also happen to be sit-com stars. You can have all the meat and cheese you want, but you can't have a slice of bread to save your life. Just go out and buy a cow, and you're all set.

My husband was skeptical. "There's no quick fix to losing weight," he said, watching me gobble up bacon, eggs, steak, and cheese. He was having a small bowl of Cheerios and some fruit (he's so unenlightened).

"That's not true," I answered, wiping grease off my chin and reaching for a pork chop, "you just see, Mister."

Two weeks later I was scared of meat. I wouldn't even pet the dog. So, I turned to a mainly liquid diet. This is very easy; you eat one sensible meal a day and have two pre-packaged drinks for the other two meals. It's also the only diet where your husband can ask what you're doing and you can answer, "Eating lunch and showering."

My goal was to be in a weight-loss commercial—twirling around on a beach somewhere and talking about how generally great I am, or shooting skeet and marveling at my own energy levels.

The truth, I've found, is simple—losing weight takes time and patience.

"You want everything now," my husband said.

"I do not!" I answered, eating a gob of raw cookie dough. "I can linger around waiting for results as well as the next person!"

So, I am exercising and eating sensibly. I know—what a drag. And I have to believe that somewhere in America, the Arrowroot cookie people are crying loudly.

THE PHANTOM AND THE PANTS

A FEW WEEKS ago I went to see *Phantom of the Opera* down in Boston at the Wang Theatre. I went with my good friend Kate, to celebrate her birthday.

Since Kate and I are both stay-at-home moms, any excursion out means a lot to us. And in truth we need them: I scared myself recently when I found that I was looking forward to going through the carwash; I found myself saving it for a "special day"; I wore new earrings. That kind of thing scares a gal.

So, I anxiously awaited the evening of the play for several reasons: the intrinsic beauty of the play, the emotion-laden vibratos of the principal players, but most of all because I would get to wear my velvet pants. These velvet pants are brand new, and I knew that they'd be nice to wear on an evening out.

Apparently, as well as being nice to wear, black velvet pants are excellent to make a slingshot with if you're 11 years old and bored and have a closet full of tennis balls and two friends over. It's just too bad I didn't know that when planning my outfit.

"Do these look funny?" I wondered aloud into the mirror, turning this way and that—the pants were pooling around my ankles and bagging at the knees. But I was short on time, so I just decided that it had been so long since I had dressed up that I had actually forgotten what was fashionable, and when Kate came to get me I ran down the stairs in a sort of a crouch, holding up my velvet pants at the knees.

"Have a good time, girls!" my husband said, stooping over to pick up tennis balls that were dropping in my wake.

"Oh, we will," we chuckled happily, each grabbing a velvet pant leg and making a run for the car. As we drove downtown, we ruminated on the majesty of the theater.

"Theater is just so—what's the word—civilized," I intoned, finishing a Yoo-Hoo I found in the middle compartment of her car and looking in my pocketbook for a Mento or TicTac.

"Your pants are growing," she replied, and sure enough, the bottoms seemed to be even with the glove box while the crotch was somewhere around my calves. "Try rolling them up." Have you ever tried to roll velvet in an upward direction? Try rolling running water and you'll get the picture.

Our seats for the play were in Row T. The Wang is great for many reasons, one of them being that you can see from any seat. But Row T is Row T, and it's up there.

As we climbed up and up, we came to think of the lobby as "Base Camp" and Row T as "The Summit." Halfway up we hired some Sherpa guides to direct us and to hold my pants, and by Row Q we were eating dried jerky and writing in journals, rattling cowbells to keep track of each other. I once read a book written by a man who climbed Mount Everest; the real trick would be to climb Mount Everest in velvet pants once used as a slingshot.

Darkness fell and the play began. It was wonderful; and I don't want to harp on how far up we were, but the Phantom swung by on the chandelier once and I tossed him a Mento and he caught it.

All too soon it was intermission. I have to say that there were some pretty fancy people at the theater that night. By now completely disabled by my pants, I stood holding my waistband and listening to snatches of conversation.

"Mumble-mumble . . . creative coalition," . . . "mumble-mumble . . . artistic integrity," and so on.

I turned to Kate and what came out, after some thinking, was "Have you read *Highlights* lately? That old Goofus and Gallant; they'll never change."

Her swift, amusing repartee was "I know what you're saying—Gallant is just so nice, while Goofus remains so rude."

Culture really is for everyone.

One thing I learned at the theater is that it's pretty easy to start a trend. As I looked around, I noticed several other patrons chatting and holding their waistbands, too. *Neat*, I thought. I put my playbill on my head, like a silly hat. So did they. I hopped on one foot. So did they.

At the end of intermission we all swept back to our seats with our coats on inside-out and our shoes on the wrong feet. We loved the play.

In the darkness of live theater, ordinary spirits swell and for a few hours we are more than our mortgages, our jobs, and our unending commitments. Longing is celebrated.

And if the Wang Theatre ever needs a new velvet awning, they know just who to call.

CR

TEN POUNDS OF MASHED POTATOES

M Y HUSBAND AND I were entertaining a friend one evening when our friend mentioned an upcoming trip to Aruba he was leaving on soon. My kids were in the other room playing with his dog, a black Lab named Gus, which he had brought along.

"Who's watching Gus while you're away?" I asked, as we all stood around the kitchen enjoying a beverage.

"Oh, he'll probably go to the kennel; he's been there before," our friend replied.

"He should stay here, with us. I'll watch him!" I bleated out, flushed with the fun of entertaining, the contentment of my kids in the other room, and visions of romping with Gus and my dog, Brandy, down at the park.

My husband's glass froze on his lips and I heard him emanate a deep, surprised, grunting sound kind of like strangling.

Our friend laughed. "Oh, no, I'm afraid he's a lot of work," he said quickly.

As my husband's smile froze to a glacier-like state and he tried to turn my lips to stone with an X-ray death stare, I avoided looking in his direction and pressed on.

"Please—it will be fun! Look how well the dogs get along!" As we peered into the living room, Brandy, a bewildered look on her face, was watching the 800-pound Gus heave himself onto a sofa.

The kids were looking on, quietly impressed by the

ensuing chaos as Gus playfully pushed all the cushions off the sofa, knocking a vase of flowers onto the floor. I shrugged and laughed as if I was often entertained by breaking glassware.

And so, at my insistence, Gus came to live with us for a week. Some of us have an almost psychotic need to please, to help out, to over-extend.

This kind of thing also happened when we prepared to move to this town about a year and a half ago. That was a very hard move for me to make. I was proud of the way I was bravely making the best of it for my kids' sakes . . . . Okay, so I did hug every tree in my old backyard before we left, and maybe I did carve all our names into the aluminum siding on our old garage, but otherwise I was pretty adult about the whole thing.

Two days before this traumatic move to Massachusetts, as I was alternately packing and sobbing, the phone rang. It was a Room Mother from my boys' elementary school who, though fully aware of my move in two days, was calling to see if I could bring ten pounds of mashed potatoes to class for a party the next afternoon. Ten pounds of mashed potatoes.

"Sure—be glad to!" I screamed into the phone, hanging it up and throwing it into an open box. And mash those potatoes I did, temporarily abandoning my packing long enough to lug them in the next day, showing up with bubble wrap in my hair and "FRAGILE" packing stickers trailing from my sneakers.

Never again will I be a doormat, I muttered to myself as I picked tiny lumps out of a child's mashed potatoes with a milk straw. *Ten pounds of mashed potatoes!*

I used to be worse. When I was nine months pregnant with my first child, I met a woman in a jewelry store who was also nine months pregnant. I learned through our conversation that she was concerned that her husband, who worked nights, would be unavailable when she went into labor.

Guess who offered to drive her to the hospital? The stranger in front of her who didn't seem to realize that possibly the woman had other relatives in the world who would be willing to help her out.

My mother made me call her and withdraw my offer toute de suite when she found out.

Ten pounds of mashed potatoes.

It's just a matter of growing up, of learning about your own value, and learning to say *no.* I am making significant progress—the other day in the grocery store a stock boy asked for some help in unloading canned goods as I passed by with my cart, and I coolly told him I didn't feel I had the time right then.

And is this trait all bad? So I sat people at my own wedding; at its origin, this eagerness to help stems from a real interest in humanity.

And you know what I say to myself whenever I am tempted to carry this line of thinking too far? *Ten pounds of mashed potatoes!*

∝

P M S

MEN AND WOMEN are different. This fact we can count on, no matter how modern we think we're getting. We've always been different; why, even back in the caveman days men were loathe to ask other cavemen for directions to the annual wildebeest hunt; and even then women were still considering throwing "rock and twig" parties, which of course evolved into the modern-day Tupperware or basket party.

Nowhere are women more different from men than in our physiological make-up. Women are, at certain times in their lives, at the mercy of their hormones.

Hormones are little pieces of matter made up mainly of barbed wire, itching powder and hot lava that run through the human body and cause certain nightmarish effects to happen at random and without explanation.

Of course, when you're in your twenties you don't believe that, because you haven't gotten hit by them full-force yet. When I was in my twenties, my new husband and I sped down the road in his little sports car as I shouted into the wind, "They've come up with yet another malady we women are supposed to suffer from, honey! It's called PMS—what a hoax! Don't worry—I'll be the same old me forever!"

Guess what. The sports car is gone, replaced by three kids, a mortgage, and a yard full of dirt that won't grow grass for some reason. And I believe in PMS. We named our first cat Midol.

The hard thing about PMS is that it sneaks up on you and, therefore, your family as well.

Take the first symptom of PMS, which professional doctors call Unreasonable Exaggeration of Grievances. It works like this: a few months back my three boys and my husband were innocently eating their breakfasts and discussing the previous night's ball game when I appeared in all my bloated glory. I had somehow, by the mere act of sleeping, gained thirty pounds in water-weight, and my pajamas were cutting off my circulation.

"So," I hissed, standing in the doorway in my bathrobe, "I noticed something interesting this morning."

Now, at this point the family members look at each

other warily. *What will it be?* their looks say.

"I noticed," I continued, circling all of them like Inspector Poirot in the drawing room with all the usual suspects, "that the recycle bins are still on the porch and the recycle trucks came a full two days ago." I approach the kids, who are looking at their dad.

Now, I should stop right here and explain to you my mindset: at that time, under the direct influence of hormones, recycle bins have taken on, in my mind, the same importance as, oh, my family setting the drapes on fire and leaving the house. There are no longer various levels of insult; it's just all bad.

After my two-hour lecture on the importance of proper recycle-bin curbside management, they got my message, I'm sure.

Another symptom of PMS is called Uncontrollable Scary Eating. This is when the PMS sufferer literally cannot get enough to eat.

Women understand this when they're together; it is not unusual for one woman to sympathetically hand another woman a pound cake during this time and not expect to have any left over for herself.

"I need to run out," I said urgently a few months ago, grabbing my keys and wallet.

"What is it, honey?" my husband asked. "Did we forget to mail the mortgage payment? Is a kid waiting alone at a ball field somewhere?"

"I forgot to buy Halloween candy," I said, heading for the door.

"It's August, though," my husband foolishly said.

"Look," I said, whirling around, "if you're comfortable waiting until the last minute to get candy and risk disappointing all the little ghosts and goblins in the neighborhood, then that's your business." I apologized later through a mouth filled with Kit Kats.

The last symptom of PMS is called Ancient Wrongs Phenomenon.

"I see you," I shrieked at my husband during the throes of PMS recently, as he was sneaking along the side of the house in a black turtleneck, black pants and night-vision goggles with a gym bag tucked under his arm—(trying to get to the YMCA to avoid my hormones, no doubt).

"Do you remember the time," I huffed, hitching up my sweatpants and advancing towards him slowly, "right before we moved here, that I asked you to pull that old rose bush out of the ground, the one I loved, so we could transplant it here? Do you know how hurt I was when you wouldn't do that one tiny thing?"

"That was four years ago, and I wouldn't do it because the bush belonged to the neighbors," he replied patiently (he's been through PMS a few times). "We knew that because it was climbing up the side of their house."

"Oh, you're so technical about everything," I snuffled, wandering off in search of food.

So, the best thing a PMS sufferer can do is to give everyone a break and go off by herself, preferably to a desert or mountaintop place where the chance of interaction with others is minimum.

The best thing her family can do is to bring in the recycle bins properly.

CR

3 ଔଔ

THESE TIMES

"Communication today is faster, slicker and more baffling than at any other time in history. We have more ways to communicate and less to talk about than ever before—it's an exciting time."

ଔ

EMERGENCY ROOM

ON A RECENT weekend, my 12-year-old preteen delight fell while doing stunts on his inline skates, necessitating a trip to the emergency room. Leaving mournful grandparents in the driveway, the whole family sped off at extremely high speeds to obtain an X-ray. I have never traveled so fast to wait so long in my entire life.

Upon arrival at the hospital, my sons were baffled by the apparently mandatory IV-patient-smoking-a-cigarette-on-the-sidewalk as we passed through the pressurized doors. They worried over this patient strolling around and puffing away, dragging his IV pole behind him. They looked to their dad, who whispered, "Don't judge. Your mother orders 'pizza with the works' and a Diet Coke all the time. Same concept."

We signed in, and went to sit down. We were soon called to "triage," the first step of the emergency room process.

My son sat down, cradling his elbow, while I hung out uncertainly at the curtain that separated us from the general populace. Twelve is a tricky age for the parent; should I talk to the medical people, or should he? Should I be inside the curtain or lurk around the outside? I opted for inside the curtain.

I have a little problem when I get into medical situations—I think that I am a doctor. While the nurse examined my son's elbow I wondered aloud whether we should order a CBC and a Chem-7. (They order this on *ER* whether you come in for a heart attack or an impacted toenail.) I looked hopefully at the box of rubber gloves, but the nurse shook her head and directed us to "registration," the next step of the process.

The nice lady at registration asked us questions while she tapped out our answers on her keyboard. Then the question was asked that throws the ER visitor just when he feels a bit confident that things will be okay.

"Your religion, please? If you'd care to state it." Whoa—what's this? This makes the patient very nervous: *could I die from this shin splint? Has anyone ever died from a sprained wrist?* My son looked intrigued, as if he were picturing a priest solemnly whispering prayers into his elbow.

We were then sent out to wait. Still being in my medical mode, I silently evaluated the room. Okay, we were probably after the toddler with the goose egg on his forehead, but we were definitely before the kid playing

"Batman" with the drapes. I noticed other patients doing the same calculations—they were smiling, but their eyes were narrowed in evaluation.

"Could you look a little more hurt?" I asked my son. "It might help."

The wait was excruciating, but I have to say I was learning a lot about myself in this down time. For example, my name backwards is "Erdried Yllier," I can count ceiling tiles in groups of up to four, and I like both Doritos and Cheetos.

During hour two my youngest son leaned over to me and whispered, "This place is a nightmare, Mom. Everyone here is hurt!" (He gets that "sharp as a tack" thing from his mother.)

A grown woman was sprawled out on the floor paying way too much attention to a beaded abacus toy she found in the corner, and my husband was voraciously reading a *Highlights* magazine, tears of boredom dropping from his eyes.

Everywhere I looked men were patiently trailing after their wives while holding their wives' purses—something I think should be started as a custom.

The nurse finally called our name, and I could feel on our backs the resentment from the room as we walked through the swinging doors. We were getting excited, though—we might see a real doctor soon!

How young we were then. They were just giving us a new setting in which to wait. Put in a small curtained cubicle, our hopes waned. I played with my hair using the metal paper towel dispenser as a mirror while my son, who is a Band-Aid fanatic, looked for wounds on his body that he could bandage. When the doctor arrived I was asleep on the examination table and my son resembled a mummy.

My son was sent to X-ray, and I was directed to the

X-ray waiting room. Nearly delirious from too much waiting and suffering from the equivalent of bedsores, I started up a lopsided conversation with a sedated patient who grinned sleepily at me while I ran through my childhood history and brought him up to my present-day activities. He seemed to think I did do the right thing when I switched majors in college back in 1979.

My son returned, and we were shuffled back out to the second waiting room, which we affectionately thought of as a kind of a summer rental.

My son was pronounced fine and given a sling, which he was thrilled about—in seventh grade, injuries mean instant, if fleeting, celebrity.

Back out to the first waiting room, where my husband was curled up fast asleep and my youngest son was mastering a wheelchair, we had a teary reunion and then turned to leave.

As we walked away, I turned to my husband. "Could you hold this?" I asked, thrusting my purse at him.

"Why?" he responded, taking the bag.

"Don't ask me," I shrugged. "It's protocol here." And off we went.

ଔ

THE IDIOT BOX

MY FAMILY AND I have been privately grappling with a situation here at home that we have had to keep to ourselves due to the sheer intensity of it all. The fact is I have an addiction. I, the mother of the family, the only person who is at home during the day and therefore can indulge in this addiction, I'm hooked on CNN.

That's right—all news, whenever I want it, prepackaged and full of spin for my viewing pleasure. And I can't get enough. Currently being pregnant, I know all about cravings and compulsions, and this one makes my family miss the days early in the pregnancy when I longed for anything cooked in garlic.

This CNN thing started innocently enough. I stumbled on the House Judiciary Committee hearings on the possible impeachment of President Clinton. I was immediately charmed; why, the members of this committee were so nice to each other! They called each other "gentleman" and "gentle lady," and they did really polite things like "yielding back" to "the chair" any extra speaking time they ended up with.

They let young clerks sit behind them while they talked and were on TV for hours at a time, while doing nothing. I live in a world where "cool," "awesome" and "what's up!" are the formal language, so to hear people talk as they did in the days of Benjamin Franklin was really inspiring.

There was another reason I got hooked on CNN. I am the biggest political dummy of all time. (It took me years to realize that "Independent" on a voter registration card was, in fact, a political affiliation. The cardholder was not, as I had thought, being just the teensy weensiest bit of a showoff about a personal character trait.) I have been known to vote for someone on the sole rationale that "with a name like that, he must be a good guy. I'm going to pull the lever now." I'm still not sure how Maria Shriver is related to the Kennedys, exactly.

With CNN I am allowed to learn about government in the privacy of my own home. Plus, being pregnant, I really like staying motionless for hours at a time and not being deemed lazy.

"Honey, we should flip you over, you're going to get couch sores," my husband once said, to which I responded, "I'm watching democracy in action here, do you mind?"

I decided we could use a little more of this politeness and decorum in our own family, so I took it on myself to impose it on my two boys. Okay, so maybe the gavel at the dinner table was a bit much. But I was determined to show them that there is another way besides "this is so lame" to cast a dissenting vote. I started with my youngest and most malleable child.

"Mom?" he said one evening, wandering into the kitchen.

"The chair recognizes the gentleman from the messy upstairs bedroom," I answered, standing at the stove. He looked at me quizzically.

"Um . . . the dog spit up in the living room," he answered, backing out of the room.

"Would you like to yield back the balance of your time?" I shouted after him.

My preteen is not so understanding. "Could you just yell at us like all the other moms, instead of hanging out the door screaming 'point of order'?" he asked. "You have lost it, Mom. Say, would you like some garlic?" To which I answered huffily, "I move to strike your last word."

I was quickly being lost to all in my little CNN world.

"I'm a little worried about Chairman Hyde," I fretted to my husband one night, as the committee hearings dragged on into the late hours. "He seems tired. I do believe, though, that Lindsey Graham of South Carolina changed his tie during the dinner break."

My husband took my chin in his hands and turned my glazed eyes to meet his. "Hello in there! You do realize, don't you, that you don't actually know these people. They're stuck in the TV." He knocked on the glass covering the TV screen. "See? They can't hear you."

He turned the television off as I winced.

"No *Larry King Live*; is that what you're saying?" I answered, as my brain dripped out of my ears. "No *Talk Back Live*? No weather reports on the half-hour? No stock market reports, . . . " I babbled on incoherently, sleep-deprived and loving it. He made me go to bed.

I am trying to tone down my CNN compulsion, but it's hard. Watching democracy in action really puts a dent in things like laundry, cleaning, and being a part of the human race.

My husband actually wanted me to quit cold turkey just because I suggested "Wolf Blitzer Reilly" for a name if our baby is a boy.

But I have to listen to my husband—he's a ranking member of our House.

CR

ATM MADNESS

A SUBTLE CHANGE has occurred in my life over the last two or three years; in fact it has been so subtle that for the longest time I couldn't even define it. It has finally hit me—the bank. I don't know anyone at my current bank, thanks largely to the invention of the ATM card.

Now, I remember in the town where I used to live I loved going to the bank, and it wasn't just for the free candy. The tellers would ask me how I was doing, comment on the size of my kids, and discreetly help me with overdrafts (I think I am the only bank customer in North America for whom overdraft protection is mandatory, as deemed by special state law). In today's world, my bank and I really have nothing to do with one another, except for the fact that they're holding all the money I have in this world, and I use their parking spaces whenever possible.

A trip to the bank now goes something like this: I stand in line and wait to be called. I am waved up to a teller's window. To identify myself, I am asked to "Please swipe your card." Recently, when asked that, I looked at the teller in horror. "It's gone," I answered, feeling the chain around my neck where I keep my ATM card. "What do we do now? What's the protocol?"

"I don't know," she whispered, easing off of her stool. "Let me get my manager."

The manager was baffled, too. "How do we know you are who you say you are?" he asked nicely.

"Look," I answered, "I have a license, ten billion credit cards, those kids over there know me but are ignoring me—so you know I'm their mom; what else can I show you?"

"Let me just get your file," he answered, walking away. Banks may start charging customers for this satisfying human contact.

A couple of months ago I wrote a check for some purchases in a local department store. The young clerk took it and stared at it with great interest. "A check," he said excitedly. "I've heard of these, but have never actually seen anyone use one—I thought you had to go downtown for that." The clerk looked over at me. "Do you know that people use ATM cards now? Also, it's hard to find leaded gas anymore, and they had to cancel *Miami Vice* some years back," he finished regretfully.

When using ATM cards, it is of paramount importance to record your purchases and withdrawals. My wallet looks like a leather submarine sandwich thanks to stacks of fluttering white ATM receipts jammed into it.

Leaving the store the other day, my nine-year-old stopped dead in his tracks. "Mom, shouldn't you record that transaction immediately in the checkbook, noting the date, amount, and location of your purchase?" he inquired, watching me stuff the receipt in my pocket.

"You are your father's son," I answered, guiltily withdrawing my receipt.

Another thing that has invaded my life is something called "online banking." My husband can now balance our checkbook on the computer, something he was initially very excited about. I couldn't share his enthusiasm since you need a computer to do it; I still refer to our home computer as "the TV that doesn't work."

Frankly, I don't think that this "online banking" is very good for him. He disappears into the computer room for a couple of hours and the kids line up at the door holding towels, Gatorade, and a wristwatch to take his pulse. I like to straighten up a different corner of the attic each time he does his work.

He finally emerges holding the bane of my life: a computer printout or "statement of activity"—a recorded tally of all our spending.

"What . . . where . . . not recorded anywhere," he gasps, groping for a chair. The kids towel him off while I go and get my receipts, making a mental note to unplug the computer and bend the prongs that go into the outlet into unrecognizable shapes.

We are so dependent on ATM machines that they can ruin a night out. Recently, all dressed up, perfumed and cologned, ready for dinner and a movie, we rolled up to the ATM machine. The screen told us that regretfully this particular machine was being serviced (as no one was there, apparently by little repair gnomes that fit inside the ATM machine itself). My husband squinted at the screen and then looked at me.

"Where's another ATM machine?"

"I don't know," I answered, starting to feel edgy. We had three dollars in cash between us, plus six corroded pennies from under the car seats. To make a long story short, we charged our movie tickets and split a McDonald's Value Meal.

I am determined not to let my life be ruled by an ATM card. I will continue to write checks, and I'm going to make a point to get to know at least one teller at my bank.

I'll be so non-dependent on ATM cards that when Y2K hits, and everyone panics, I'll be cool as a cucumber, sitting back and eating my Value Meal, proudly paid for with hundreds of rusted coins.

COMMUNICATION THEORY

I ONCE HAD a job telemarketing—the most thankless job on the planet. A girlfriend and I spent long hours listening to people hang up on us as we tried to sell our product—the then brand-new cellular car phone.

Prospective customers said things to us like "you mean you think that I'm gonna drive my car and talk on the phone at the same time? What are you, sick?" And so on.

"These people are right," I whispered to my girlfriend as we sat in a meeting where stock in the company was being offered, "this cell phone thing is never going to fly."

Guess what! It did fly—communication today is faster, slicker and more baffling than at any other time in history. We have more ways to communicate and less to talk about than ever before—it is an exciting time.

Almost everyone I know has a cell phone, and mostly when people call me it's to tell me that they can't talk.

"Honey, it's me," my husband will say when I pick up the phone. "I can't talk to you right now; I'm heading out of range. I just wanted to say hi. Goodbye!"

I look at our baby, who looks at me. "I thought I heard seagulls," I explain. "He must be near water."

My parents just got two cell phones—they call me from Maryland to tell me that they can't talk to me. "We have limited minutes," my mother will shout into the phone, "so I'm calling to tell you we'll call you back later. Goodbye, now!"

No matter how good the technology is, sometimes you lose your cellular connection when the actual cells in the phone cannot bounce off the right planets up in outer space (at least this is how I used to explain it to prospective customers). A friend will call you from her cell phone and shout over the sounds of mall traffic, ". . . you won't believe it! (Small Coke, please.) I finally learned at the retreat last weekend (Could I have a straw?) that the meaning of life, the very purpose of our existence is . . . . "

A few minutes later you can be sure that she will suddenly be outside a "roaming area," guaranteeing that you will be "frustrated beyond all belief."

Another method of instant communication is e-mail via computer. My mother and I were excited when she got a computer; "We'll e-mail each other all the time and it will be free!" we crowed to each other. The problem, though, is that a few minutes after posting an e-mail to her I would end up calling her on the phone.

"Have you checked your e-mail?" I would ask. "Oh, no? Well, here's what I told you in the e-mail . . . " and thus another thirty-dollar phone call would be triumphantly launched.

One of the most frustrating forms of modern communication is the telephone answering machine—mainly because I am part of a fringe group in our society that turns into total babbling idiots when they know they're being recorded. Here's me leaving a message:

"Hi, it's Deirdre. You're not home, are you! Well, of course you're not, otherwise I would be talking to you! (Dead air where you can hear me thinking) Anyway, I just wanted to know if . . . is that you picking up? Oh, I guess not . . . you know how sometimes you think someone's picking up but they're not? (Coughing and gagging sounds) Excuse me! Anyway, just call me back when you have a second—did I say this was Deirdre? Well, it's me, so call me back. Thanks a lot! Okay, bye!"

And that's just me calling the plumber. You should hear what it's like when calling a friend.

In this age of instant communication it's never been more difficult to actually reach someone. The moment my husband leaves for work he becomes an almost mythical figure—we know we're not going to be able to talk to him unless he checks in with us. It's as if he steps off our front porch and is instantly transported in his business suit to the deepest jungles of the Amazon—you cannot get the man on the phone.

He has voicemail—this is a number you can call to hear what day it is, where he is, and an assurance that he'll get back to you. I've learned that if you leave a message like, "I'm sitting here folding laundry and questioning every concept I've always held true about the meaning of my life in this great, vast universe, and just wondering basically about my place in the big scheme of things, metaphorically speaking, of course," it will take him a really long time to call you back.

We are on the brink of great things in communication; you can just vaguely feel it: wireless this-and-that, digital this-and-that, and so many new devices!

We were at a restaurant the other day and it was like sitting with a bunch of gunslingers—people creeping to their tables loaded down with all manner of cell phone, beeper and vibrating restaurant pager.

Over lunch my husband was telling me that soon we'll all have phones with little TV screens so that we can see who we're talking to.

I just laughed. That will never fly, I explained confidently. Women in particular are going to be stuck in the bathroom all day doing their hair in case the phone rings!

My husband immediately excused himself—I'm not sure, but I think he was going to go buy some stock. ଔଔ

SCHOOL VACATION ISLAND

I N THE WAKE of the fantastic ratings success of "reality" shows such as *The Mole, Survivor* and *Temptation Island*, the savviest TV producers in the business have devised a reality show for kids, specifically teens, who are at a significant age developmentally—but even more important, are at their peak purchasing power. The producers have decided to test it on you, the heralded TV viewer. The name of the show: *School Vacation Island.*

(Fade in: A handsome, tanned man, dressed in a safari suit, peeks out from behind some old Rubbermaid trashcans on an average, ordinary street and begins speaking in a whisper, glancing around as he does.)

Flip.   Hello, there, America! This is Flip Flop, your host for *School Vacation Island,* and I will do just about anything for ratings! All right! Let me explain how *School Vacation Island* works: inside this average home lives an average family—a mom, a dad, a teenage son, a preteen son, and a baby son, not quite two. However, we won't focus on the baby because, let's face it, he's barely a demographic yet!

Anyway, the challenge goes out to the two older sons. Here's the setup—it's February vacation, everyone this family knows is at Disneyland, the dad couldn't get any time off from work, the car broke down, and there's not a nutritious speck of food in the house. The challenge is for our boys to enjoy their February vacation! And with any luck, they'll disavow one another right here on national TV! Let's meet them now.

(Pan to Flip Flop waving frantically to two boys walking down the driveway in their sleeping clothes.)

Flip. Hey, boys, it's Flip Flop! Come on over here and crouch behind your trash cans and let us know how vacation is going!

Oldest Boy. Well, Flip, we actually just got up. We make it a policy to stay in bed to at least noon on vacation—then we get up and eat Pop Tarts and lie back down on the couch.

Flip. Are you ready to disavow one another?

Oldest Boy. Not quite yet, Flip. We are ready to try to get a ride to the mall, though.

Flip. Teerrific! You are quite the competitors. Let's just hope tensions don't mount. Your assignment, boys, is to go get that ride from your mom, and also to very stealthily go down to the basement and identify whose clothes are in the washing machine. We call this the 'Utility Challenge.' Our inside intelligence tells us that the wash has been forgotten there for two days at least. If you are successful, I'll hand you this worthless totem pole thing, and you'll both be allowed to stay on *School Vacation Island.*

Youngest Boy (Uncertainly). But we live here, Flip.

Flip. So right! Run along now while we take a camera and try to see what Mom is doing!

(Fade in)

Flip. We're back, folks, and here come our boys now! Let's see how they did. Boys, did you get that ride, and identify the wash?

Oldest Boy. Flip, our mom said that the car is making a funny noise, and she doesn't trust it. But a friend's mom is going to take us. As for the laundry, it's the baby's stuff. We told our mom, who said thank you very much, but she's well aware that she has laundry that has dried inside the washer.

Flip. Well done, boys. Any hint of trouble between you two—are you ready to disavow each other yet?

Oldest Boy. No, Flip, but we've hit a wrinkle. Mom wants us to get some of our homework done early, so we don't save it for Sunday night.

Flip. Oooh! That's a tough one—and she looks so nice; we can see her through the window, sitting there knitting.

Youngest Boy. Actually, Flip, she's sticking pins in a Mickey Mouse doll.

Flip. Well, at any rate, you've won the worthless totem pole thing, and that moves you up into our double-secret, double-dare round. If you have the guts, the stamina, the belief in something greater than yourselves, but ESPECIALLY if you look good on TV, we are prepared to offer you whole careers in the entertainment business, as well as commercial endorsements totaling millions! Of course, if you disavowed each other, that would help.

Oldest Boy. Sorry, Flip—we'd really just like to avoid our homework, relax, and get to the mall.

Flip. Just tell on each other, a harsh word, a spitball, anything . . . arrgh . . . .

(Flip twirls away out of sight, devastated that his pilot show, already hyped in the press, really was just about February vacation. [He does go on, however, to win a lucrative endorsement contract from Chapstick.]

(The two boys turn and walk inside, where they remove a tattered Mickey Mouse doll from their mom's grasp.)

—Fade out—

CR

PILL POPPER

L ATELY, THERE IS a new demographic of the population that I have increasing respect for, especially since I have temporarily joined them. These are the people in our society who are on daily multiple medications. Be they senior citizens, people with chronic health problems or people like me—pregnant and sick with flu—they get a tip of the hat from me.

How do these people find time to eat, sleep, and breathe? Right now I am on a few different vitamins and medications and am always either waiting to take a pill, taking a pill, or getting over taking a pill.

One problem is timing. I have one medication that must be taken one hour before breakfast and a prenatal vitamin the size of a Chicken McNugget that should be taken with food.

Then I have two supplemental iron pills that are taken separately with food but not with milk. And, for a short time, an antibiotic that must be taken three times a day. Because of the side effect of the antibiotic, I have to hover around the bathroom for about an hour after each pill.

A friend called the other day to see if I could go to the bookstore with her.

"Let's see," I mused, organizing my pills on the counter. "I need to take a pill at 10:35, another at 11:00, and in between I've scheduled some probable bathroom time. I can pencil you in from 11:15 to 11:35, though, as long as you don't plan on stopping for anything made with dairy products."

"Call me back when you have the baby," she answered, hanging up.

Another problem is actually getting into the medication or vitamin pill. Presumably, using the same plastic that is used to protect the rocket boosters on the space shuttle, today's medicine is packaged for descendants of Houdini. After gnawing on an entombed iron caplet, trying to pry it open with a steak knife and giving it to the dog to work on, I handed it to my boys.

"Could you find the highest vertical spot in this house, go to it, and drop this?" I asked.

One evening my kids and I were watching television when a commercial came on advertising a new drug used for a relatively minor health problem.

"Turn that up," I said excitedly to the boys. "Your Uncle Ray has that problem. Maybe this medication could help." We watched as two disgustingly healthy people floated into view, and a voice told us all about this exciting new drug.

Near the end of the commercial the voice said, somewhat regretfully, "This medication, although safe for some, is not for everyone. Anyone pregnant or nursing should not take this medication. Also, anyone who has high blood pressure, heart disease, or has a history of coughing, sneezing or deep breathing should not take this medication. Additionally, anyone who needs to stand upright, use their hands to grasp, or hold down part-time or full-time employment should not take this medication.

"Side effects, though rare, include blurred vision, difficulty breathing, spontaneous hair loss, tonsil enlargement, rapid-fire flatulence, drying of the eyeballs, and sudden lurching. Talk to your doctor . . . walk in the sun . . . take as directed."

My boys looked at me suspiciously. "Don't we like

Uncle Ray anymore?" they asked.

Over-the-counter medications can be iffy, too. My sister once took a nighttime medication for a bad cold. A few minutes after she ingested it, she started exhibiting some pretty spaced-out behavior.

"How are you feeling?" I asked, sensing that she was having side effects.

"Beige," she answered dreamily, kissing her elbow. I made her get over that particular cold the old fashioned way—plenty of hot tea and tissues.

Picking up your medication can be a challenge. Let's face it, there are some medical conditions you'd rather keep to yourself while dealing with them.

One time I was in the pharmacy waiting to pick up a prescription when I heard an acquaintance say, "Deirdre, is that you in the trench coat and sunglasses? How are you . . . are you wearing a fedora? You look just like Ingrid Bergman in *Casablanca*," she giggled.

Just then the pharmacist leaned over the counter, and, grabbing a bullhorn, shouted, "Mrs. Reilly, your prescription is ready. This medication should take care of your sweating, diarrhea, and Teletubbies hallucinations." Now, that is information I could've kept to myself.

So, to those of you who deal with this and much more in the pursuit of good health, I salute you. Now please, go take your medicine.

CB

THERE ARE THINGS
I FORGOT TO TELL YOU . . .

A FEW DAYS ago, I saw the need to take my two
older boys, ages 11 and 14, school shopping.
They had been asking for new school clothes the last
few weeks of summer, but as I sent them off to the
first day of school in their bathing suits with a towel
slung over their shoulders I cautioned, "Don't buy into
the hype! These stores want you to think that you
have to have new clothes to be 'in'! We'll buy our new
clothes this year in dribs and drabs."

Well, dribs and drabs just wasn't going to cut it—
when your kid can't get his head through the neck-
hole of his tee shirt and he's wearing a rope for a belt
like Jethro Bodeen, it's probably time to go shopping.

The day of the shopping trip I was exhausted, having been up with a teething baby the whole night before. Another unfortunate factor for the boys was that I
had spent my time awake in the night watching re-runs
of *The Waltons* on cable. *The Waltons* was a '70s show
on TV about a Depression-era family with a bunch of
kids who lived in the mountains of somewhere or other.
And this was a *Walton* marathon, to be exact.

Now, you do not want to be school shopping with
your mom when she had been watching *The Waltons*
all night. My older son presented me with a shirt he
wanted. I peered at the price tag mumbling, "When
John-Boy Walton had to choose between a suit of
clothes to wear to graduation or his family's very survival due to the fact that their cow 'Chance' had died, I

don't think he was worried about a fancy shirt to wear. Do you?"

My son looked at me speculatively and said, "Huh," putting the shirt in our cart.

"The Waltons didn't need a high-falutin' mall to shop at," I said to the baby, who was grunting with the effort of trying to climb out of the cart. "They were just happy for what they had."

My mood worsened when my younger son presented me with a pair of expensive sneakers.

"Do you think when Jim Bob was pinned under the Model T car his thoughts were about what was on his feet?" I asked, hearing myself start to get irrational (like Corabeth Godsey, the shopkeeper on Walton's mountain could be, when pressured). My son wandered away, choosing wisely not to become involved.

As moms walked by loaded down with designer duds, and their kids looked like Universal Studios tour guides as they directed them down the aisles, I watched the baby run through racks of clothes enjoying the feel of price tags on his head.

"Tomfoolery," I muttered, checking my pocket watch.

As we were in line with our purchases, my kids asked me if we could grab some lunch.

"Perhaps we'll just grab some cornmeal, grind it down, make it into some bread, and cook it on an old-fashioned stove like Ma Walton had to do," I said grumpily. It was then that my kids pointed out that I had managed to get two blouses, a frame, and a lamp into the cart (hey, even the Waltons upgraded their furniture as times got better).

As my kids walked in front of me, I thought that in spite of the difference in era, how much like the Waltons my kids were—just boys trying to navigate through an ever-changing world, trying to fit in and yet stand alone at the same time.

I remember my oldest son's first day of kindergarten. As he got ready to walk into his classroom without me for the first time, I felt panicked. "Wait!" I wanted to shout after him. "There are things I forgot to tell you! Are you sure you know where the bathroom is? Will you tell someone if you feel sick? Do you remember that I'll be at home waiting for you?"

But I didn't. I said brightly, "It's going to be great, just great, pal. I'll see you soon!"

Now he's started high school this year. As he walked down the road that first day, I wanted to run after him. "Wait!" I wanted to say. "There are things I forgot to tell you! Did you know there's no one like you? Did you know that the world is opening up for you? Did you know I'll be waiting at home for you?" Instead, my coffee blurred in its cup as I said to no one, "It's going to be great—just great, pal."

Cℛ

THE SNOWSTORM

THE COMPETITORS FACED one another, squinting and adjusting their helmets. Sweat rolled down their faces as they planned their next move, pulling on their gloves and swigging down Gatorade. No, this wasn't a motor speedway or a wrestling match; this was my local supermarket just before the last big snowstorm.

In aisle 5, I wrestled with another mom for the last carton of fresh eggs. "Lay off!" she grunted. "I'm planning a pancake breakfast for my two kids when school is cancelled!"

I smirked, and tugged harder. "I'm making home made waffles for my whole family, plus I'm freezing some for later!"

She scowled and let go of the eggs; I had clearly won.

"Good luck with those waffles," she said, a true sportswoman.

"It's yours next time—I can just feel it," I responded, high-fiving her as we parted.

Next, the milk. As I headed towards the refrigerated section I saw a dad who had my number; he was coming up hot and heavy, trailing two whining kids behind him, a toddler in the cart.

Darn, I thought, adjusting my mouthpiece and spitting on the floor. Kids are always a bonus in this situation.

"Look thirsty," I heard him whisper to the toddler as we both descended on the last gallon of whole milk. I smiled at the kids and mouthed, "We'll meet again," to the victorious dad.

I wheeled my cart around, stooping down to throw some WD-40 on my brakes while I planned my next move. Bodies flew through the air as I passed by the soda aisle, and the same happened in the Duraflame section. Sadly, we all shared the same dream: throw down some rock salt, light a chemical log, swill down some Coca-Cola and let the snow fall, baby.

As we waited for the snow to start, a little-known phenomenon that has been studied in many parts of suburban Alaska began to occur—a psychological condition called Repetitive Question Dementia.

Now this, in layman's terms, is when kids literally drive their parents to the brink of insanity asking one simple question, and that question is: "Do you think we'll have school tomorrow?"

They'll flop across your bed and ask it, they'll stand outside the bathroom door and ask it, they'll hang upside down outside your bedroom window and ask it.

They don't really want to know your answer; if you say, "Yes," they'll say, "How would you know?"

Kids who drool and scratch their heads when you ask them how many fingers you're holding up suddenly become junior meteorologists, studying charts and graphs, drinking coffee, and wearing pencils behind one ear as they watch the Weather Channel for a hint as to whether they will have school off the next day.

For this last storm, the whole family ended up watching the tiny little strip on the bottom of the TV screen where they announce school closings. The kids showed the concentration of air traffic controllers as they recited the names of all the "lucky towns" and waited for their town to appear.

Now, this little strip at the bottom of the TV screen becomes somewhat hypnotic, and frustrating as well. Just as they are getting to your town's name, a commercial will come on or a power outage will occur and the whole family goes, "Oh! Now we have to watch the whole thing again!" Which we do.

In this particular storm the power went out for almost the entire day. I went from room to room all day like an idiot babbling, "Oh yeah! I can't do this!" as I tried to make coffee, blow-dry my hair, or boil hot dogs.

The kids solemnly watched the blackened TV set, speaking in hushed whispers as they stroked the screen gently and shared memories: "Remember the way it would just come right on, the minute you pushed the power button? It was always so good about that, you know?"

The kids ended up building snow forts with their friends, and we met neighbors in the street and shared laughs and groans, and all of us looked to the sky, which we almost forget to do in fair weather.

There are a few things in life that make you stop and catch your breath, and one of them is a wild, blowing snowstorm that takes your power and brings back your imagination.

With no one asking you to log on, stop by or tune in, you can hear your own heart beating in the stillness of all that white; and as you walk down a snowy lane, hearing your boots crunch the repeating, returning mystery of snow, you catch yourself smiling and whispering, "Hello there, it's so good to catch up with you"—and you're speaking to yourself.

CR

4 ∞

THE CHALLENGED COUPLE

"... I'm in kids' futures."

∞

HIGH SCHOOL REUNION

RECENTLY, MY HUSBAND and I were invited to attend the twentieth reunion of his high school class. Now, men and women view this type of thing quite differently; in his mind, he said to himself, *Great, should be fun, I'll see the old gang, wonder what's in the fridge?* while my mind, upon hearing of the invitation, went, *Oh my gosh, this is in a month? How will I lose 15 pounds by then? I can do it. What will I wear? I've got to start looking right away . . . gee, I wonder if any of his old girlfriends will be there? Where is my suede skirt, and does it fit . . . where's my Abdominizer, my ThighMaster, my control-top pantyhose and my water bottle . . . are we really this old?*

So, my big "reunion diet" started, and ended, and

started again. With one week until the reunion and no
pounds lost, I began to focus on wardrobe.

"You're taking this way too seriously," my husband commented one night, watching me look at different outfits as I flung them to the bed.

"I am not—hand me the Ace bandage and the
Vaseline," I ordered. I knew that he would show up in
a bathrobe and knee socks as long as he could social-
ize with his friends, while I would employ a crowbar
and a team of firefighters to rescue me from my dress
as long as I could wear what I wanted to wear.

The night of the reunion finally came. Our three
kids were with my in-laws—we were looking at a real
night out! Everything was going according to plan
when my husband and I both made a fatal mistake—
we sat down on the couch. You don't sit on our couch
when you're dressed up—we both know better! We
have a big dog that sheds her weight in hair each
week, and since she spends a good amount of her time
and energy sneaking up onto the couch . . . well, you
get the picture. "Ahhh!" we both yelped, jumping up,
but it was too late.

Needless to say, Mr. and Mrs. Dog Hair were late,
and stood in the lobby furiously picking dog hair off of
each other while listening to the sounds of clinking
glasses and laughter inside.

We walked through the doors and were both given
name tags (Hello! My name is Daedree Reilly) that
were adorned with a copy of my husband's senior
yearbook picture.

"You had an Afro?" I asked, as we started to min-
gle. Mingling with my husband is interesting, mainly
because he takes off the minute we arrive at any func-
tion. I don't mind—hey, I watch the guy floss his teeth
every night; some alone time is good. And I didn't have

trouble locating him; I just looked for the man in the hairy suit.

Ah, it was great to be out, even if I was in a room full of strangers, wearing a picture of my husband as a teen-ager on my chest, and listening to Bachman Turner Overdrive.

I quickly became a part of a conversational group of "spouses" standing near the bar. "And what do you do?" a smartly dressed woman about my age asked politely, snacking on a stuffed mushroom.

"Well," I answered, "I am at home with three kids . . . "

"Three!" she shrieked, "why you're like the Waltons! If you're not working, then what do you do for *you*—I mean to self-actualize?"

"Well, I try to eat right, and get plenty of rest . . . "

"I mean," she tried again, "do you do yoga? Meditate? How do you get in touch with your inner self in the thick of it all?"

I've been trying to get in touch with myself for years—I just can't get me to return my calls. Meditate? Yoga? Time is at a premium for me—I've been walking around with one eyebrow plucked for ten months since we had our baby; everyone keeps telling me I look startled.

My new friend was still at it. "Have you tried aroma-therapy? Taking a bath while smelling specifically scented candles? Have you tried that?" Was this lady on commission or something? A mental picture came to mind of my tub back home, its washcloths flung everywhere, hair in the drain, and mildew on the grout.

I shook my head regretfully. "I spend a lot of time breaking Cheerios in half for the baby, and sometimes for a creative outlet I move the den furniture around," I offered.

"*Feng shui!*" she cried, relieved, and the group said, "Bless you," and searched for a hanky.

Just then my husband showed up with a few other fellows who were all in paroxysms of laughter, apparently, from what I could piece together, from remembering a time they drove a car up a hill. (High school memories are best shared by those who were there.)

"Hon, do you want to dance?" my husband asked through a haze of dog hair.

"Well," I said doubtfully, "they're playing *Free Bird* . . . "

What the heck. We hit the dance floor, and I have to say, people cleared a circle around us, just like in the movies. I don't know if it was our obvious oneness together as we danced or the dog hair that puffed off our backs as we swayed, but high school has never looked so good.

CR

HIGH SOCIETY

D INING OUT IN high society is something that my husband and I don't do very often—we're more the type to eat with people who say "come on over and take a dip in the cee-ment pond!" My father, my husband, and I once had occasion, however, to go to a very formal dinner party, and needless to say, I learned a lot.

The dress I chose to wear to the dinner was very "in" at the time—a short dress with petticoats; a kind of Scarlett-O'Hara-meets-Bianca-Jagger look. I not so much walked into the dinner party as flounced in—to be greeted by our very gracious hostess and other guests, including women who were flouncing, too.

There are rules to formal dining, and they are as follows:

Rule #1:

You don't sit with him who brung ya.

My husband, I was disturbed to see, was placed between an older gentleman and a woman who apparently chose not to wear clothing to the dinner. Her thin gown gave her the appearance of being stark naked, while I was furiously beating my petticoats down just to get into my seat at the table.

The dinner featured Asian cuisine attractively presented on beautiful, unique tableware—in other words, I was totally out of my league. Foods I've never seen were placed before me, and I struggled to learn to use my chopsticks while checking out my dinner partners.

Rule #2:

You make engaging conversation with total strangers.

At a formal dinner, you speak to the people to your right and to your left while seated at the table. I turned to my right, where a dapper man about my age was turned toward me expectantly. "Hello," I said, introducing myself while nonchalantly trying to fling a peapod into my mouth.

"Hello, I'm in the financial field. What do you do?" he asked, smiling pleasantly.

"I'm a mom—I'm raising two small children," I said, throwing some noodles in the direction of my face. Now, interestingly enough, my answer to his question had the same effect as having bugs and worms crawling out of my eyes, ears, and nose would have—he was absolutely horrified.

Our conversation clearly being over, I looked down the long table to see how my husband was faring. The naked lady was speaking to him animatedly while he ate his dinner. I was annoyed. Since when did he know how to use chopsticks?

I turned to the gentleman on my left, who was turned toward me, waiting to talk. "Hello," he said. "I'm in cattle futures. What do you do?" Finally getting a handle on my chopsticks, I picked up a morsel of food from among the mysterious things on my plate and steered it towards my mouth, while answering, "I'm in kids' futures." A man who obviously appreciated my vocation, he looked at me in awe as I began to eat my hard-won bite of food. Unfortunately, I had picked up a decorative ceramic leaf with my chopsticks and heard my back teeth breaking before I could spit it out.

Rule # 3:

"When you've alienated your dinner partners, wing it."

If this should happen you can: (a) mentally organize your closets at home, (b) pretend that you are smiling and gesturing appreciatively at someone in another room just beyond everyone else's view, (c) see if it's true that if you cross your eyes too often, one of these times they just may stay crossed.

Rule # 4:

After-dinner conversation may be tricky if you are not with a peer group.

Standing in a small group, we discussed film (no one in my group had seen *Space Jam*), literature (no one in my group reads cereal boxes for pleasure), and financial trends (no one in my group was a coupon-clipper).

Just when I was finally feeling comfortable (translation: I was happily clinging like a dryer sheet to my husband and/or dad), it was time for us to go.

Saying our good nights, we headed out into the street

and I pulled crumbs out of my dress as we discussed the evening. My father had enjoyed the food, while my husband wondered if the waiters were eating our leftovers.

"Well, at least we were all together," I sighed.

"Were you there?" my dad asked—we were seated pretty far away from one another.

We then went to the one place where we all felt right at home—McDonald's. It's nice to know you really can go home again.

¢¢

PLAY DATE

SOME MONTHS AGO I was staring out the window of our home, watching some neighbors depart for what was obviously a fancy evening out. Dressed to kill, they swept over to their car where they sped away, no doubt for an evening chock full of class and high society. I leaned over with a groan and picked up my ninety-millionth baby toy of the day while checking out my own uniform of gym shorts and a tee shirt.

"We need some culture in our lives!" I yelled, wiping up a doggie accident with a paper towel. "We need to expand our horizons! Learn about other people from other lands! Have a night out that doesn't involve sippie cups and baby wipes! We need culture!"

"We have culture coming out our ears," my husband replied, standing by the refrigerator and guzzling Kool-Aid from a plastic container. "We have cable! Didn't you just watch that naked lady lying around on a piano and singing on PBS the other night?"

"That was Bernadette Peters, she wasn't naked, and I want to watch something cultural without having to make a pledge to buy a tote bag and beach towel. It's decided," I said, scraping burnt macaroni and cheese out of a saucepan, "we're going to get some culture!"

A couple of weeks later my husband came home from work holding an envelope. "I went to The Ticket Hut and got some tickets to a play—it's called *Rent*." He waved the envelope in the air.

"That's perfect!" I crowed exuberantly. "It's expensive, we don't know anyone in it, and it's gotten mixed reviews. We're talking real culture!"

So we planned for our night out in Boston and our trip to "the thee-ay-tah." Now, everyone knows that getting ready for the evening is almost as fun as the evening itself. I put my hair up into a fancy "chignon," which I think is the French word for "painful twisting of every hair on your head." I modernized an old bridesmaid dress when I had a few moments the week before our play (this is single-income family code for "I went out and spent a fortune on a dress I'll never wear again"), and we were ready for our night on the town.

As we sat at dinner in a fancy restaurant that evening we made some attempts to talk culture.

"So, have you ever read *A Moveable Feast* by Ernest Hemingway?" I inquired of my husband politely—in fact I was talking all through dinner as if I had never even met the guy before. I guess I was mentally ignoring the fact that only hours earlier I had seen this man I was so formally talking to change a poopy diaper wearing ski goggles in order to amuse the baby.

He looked uncomfortable. "Ah, yes, I believe I have read *A Moveable Feast* by Ernest Hemingway—I like to call him 'Hem'." He glanced around, apparently in hopes that a waiter would walk by and give him the score to some game or other.

"And what did you think of it?" I asked attentively, secretly trying to slide bobby pins back into my hair—they were popping from the back of my head at an astonishing rate.

"Hmm, now that is one good question," he stalled. "I felt that it was about a feast. A portable feast—kind of a 'Meals On Wheels' idea to it. Yes, that's what I thought."

And so on. For the rest of the dinner we stayed away from the Famous Authors category.

There is one thing that every theatergoer should remember when he or she spends a million dollars for the tickets, arranges child care for three kids, pays for parking downtown, and eats a dinner he or she will be making payments on for six months—don't be late for the actual play. Which is exactly what we were.

As we entered the lobby we were hit by the eerie stillness that enveloped us as we looked around for other theatergoers. Two very chic people (chic people often have uneven hairdos) sat outside the theater door looking as if they would arm-wrestle us to the ground before they would let us through those doors.

After a heated debate in which I explained that we thought the play started at 8:30 instead of 8:00 and bobby pins flew out of my hair, we were allowed in.

Now the trouble with seeing *Rent* is that you absolutely cannot miss the premise of the play, which to this day I do not know. As we sat in our seats watching the actors say things like, "Oh, if only we could go on living here," as they milled around what was supposed to be either an apartment building or a detention center (we would have known if we had not been late), we looked at each other in the dark.

"Do all these people live together?" he asked the audience-member to his left, who shushed him. I would have been content to watch the confusion on stage and pick bobby pins up off the floor all night, but my husband had to know what was going on.

"Are all the characters on some sort of federal assistance program?" he asked himself in frustration, ending up by turning to me and saying, "Well, at least there aren't any cats in this. Are there?"

We found culture totally exhausting, to say the least. We were more than happy to order out for Chinese food the next weekend and sit back and watch a movie on videotape.

And classy is as classy does; a few months after the *Rent* debacle we were members of the audience at one of our local middle schools for a high school drama club production of *Godspell,* and I watched in awe as the actors sang, danced, and acted their hearts out doing something they obviously loved.

Now, that's culture.

CR

MY VALENTINE

SOMETIMES THE JOB of parenting is not one of glories and triumphs, but more a job of survival. That's part of the frustration of parenting—we are not told the truth by experts. Instead of using popular buzz words like "fun," "rewarding," and "fulfilling," those in the know need to look straight at the camera and say, "Just make it to the end of the week, honey." Sometimes that, in itself, is parenting.

Now, one thing parents need to understand (and not feel bad or guilty about) is that for a long span of time, encompassing 15 or 20 years, your social, romantic, and private life is shot. You are a vehicle, a wallet, and a collect-call phone number. Friday night, back in your pre-kids days, was something to grin about, plan for, and save money on behalf of. Now, as parents, you just figure out different, new locations to be exhausted in. That's about all there is to it.

Here is an example of any Friday night lived through by myself and my husband. He calls me from his workplace, exhausted and beaten up by the week, and I say sympathetically, "If I don't get out of this loony bin tonight, I'll go insane. We're taking the kids and going out to eat, budget or no budget." (It's important to be there for one another.)

As he drives home (taking as many back roads as possible, even driving through fields), I wrestle the baby into his snowsuit and bellow up the stairs, "We're going out to eat! Turn off all cellular devices, return your tray tables to their upright positions, and meet us at the car!"

We like to go to a restaurant right in our town that is very family-friendly. Everyone there between 6 p.m. and 8 p.m. is trying to talk over kids whining, food flying, and whole families under the table trying to grab one unruly toddler. The parents' faces are not unlike the blank faces of inmates on a chain gang who have been told that the Governor was unsympathetic to their hopes of a pardon and they will keep paying for their crime forever, and ever, and ever. We join them, screaming to each other things like, "I hear that interest rates are coming down," while the baby tosses sugar packets at our heads.

The next stop is the video store. Here we pick out a movie, the kids pick out a game, and we all head to the counter where we are informed as to the late fees we have racked up that week. The grown-ups hand the clerk their wallets while saying, "What game? When did we rent that? When was it due?" while the kids visit with their friends. On the way home, we are treated to my husband's lecture entitled, "We Are Never Renting Games And Movies Again, Ever."

Next, the baby is put to bed, and my husband and I sneak upstairs to put on our rented romantic comedy. We plop into bed and immediately get unbelievably groggy. Each person pretends that they are watching the movie and not drooling their heads off.

Then, the tricky part comes. The attractive man in the movie tenderly watches the attractive woman in the movie as she sleeps, sucking in all that is beautiful and admirable about her as he gazes at her adoringly. She looks perfect and is wearing a skimpy nightie.

I roll over to face my husband, grunting with the effort of moving pounds of sweatshirt and flannel around under the covers.

"Why don't you ever watch me sleep?" I demand,

although in truth I question the idea. I'm not sure what I look like when I'm asleep, but if my crooked hair, rumpled face and bunched-up clothing come morning are any indication, he may be better off waiting until I'm awake to suck up all my great qualities.

Still, I persist. "He's looking at her like she means everything to him—why, he couldn't live one minute without her—he wouldn't even want to!"

My husband looks offended, speaking through mouthfuls of popcorn. "No one does that!" he exclaims mightily. "That's just in the movies! Don't buy into the hype!"

All too soon, the evening is at an end, usually with the baby in the bed with us, his baby feet in our faces, and kids who stay up later than we do are wrestling downstairs.

My husband, not making it through the movie, is unconscious beside me in a puddle of popcorn, his day finally ended, another one just like it around the next bend.

And I watch him sleep.

CR

5 ☙☙

OPPORTUNITY KNOCKS

---

*"They soon had the most beautiful castle in
the land, and it was admired by all, but
inside they roamed the halls separately,
and inside it was quiet."*

ॐ

REAL ESTATE TYCOON

EVERY MARRIED COUPLE has a period in their
lives that they'd just as soon forget about—maybe
it was the time that the Christmas lights stayed up all
year, or maybe it was the time that the rented movie in
its obvious white box was returned after a month of being avoided as it sat in plain view on the coffee table.

For my husband and me, in addition to those listed
above, it's got to be the time, early in our marriage,
when I decided that we should become real estate ty-
coons because a nice man with an infomercial said
that we could.

Okay, we were young. And we were broke—our
money had stretch marks on it. And we had a new

baby, so you could say our defenses were down. And, most importantly, we knew you didn't need a dumb old real estate license to sell real estate—you just needed a Hawaiian shirt and a dream.

This all came about because we were up very late one night with a cranky baby. My husband was turning the channels on the TV manually (we couldn't afford a remote control) and finishing a world-class Spam sandwich.

"Good Spam sandwich, honey," he said, sighing. "How's the baby?"

"Good," I said. "What time is it?"

"Uh, 3:30 a.m. . . . say, did you clean the windows today? I feel like I can see the actual root system of a shrub out there!" (We lived in a basement apartment that I believe now is being used as a lab where they do experiments involving mice and light deprivation.)

"Yes, I did. Say, look at that guy on TV. Look at that beach and those palm trees. Look at those happy people sitting with him. Turn that up, honey."

The handsome tanned man on the screen peered out at us from behind a frenzy of palm fronds and smiled at us. I smiled back. As the sound came on, I heard the man say over the sounds of the ocean and the seagulls (who amazingly enough were wearing little diamond anklets on their little tiny legs)—". . . why, maybe you're even sitting in your tiny basement apartment, perhaps nursing a sick child or something . . . ."

I looked over at my husband and said, "Jeepers."

"And maybe," he continued, "you've been wondering if there will ever be a day that you can just stop eating all that Spam and live a little—pursue your dreams, perhaps paint or do sculpture in the morning . . ."

"Jeepers!" I said again. "It's like he knows us. Who is he?" My eyes were receding into the back of my head like raisins, I was so tired, but this guy had my attention.

"Perhaps you're saying, 'Who is this guy?'" A gust of wind blew his handlebar moustache all around, and the deliriously happy people sitting next to him giggled wealthily. "Well, please meet the McFibbers, my extremely close personal friends who I recently had the pleasure of meeting for the first time. Now, John and Molly, tell us about yourselves while I listen to you with a fascinated expression on my face."

"Well, thanks, friend. I'll tell you, we used to be real wrecks," the man chuckled in remembrance. "I was a full-time blood donor, and the little lady here," he motioned over to the incredibly happy Mrs. McFibber, who was batting palm fronds out of her way, "she had her hands full feeding me cookies and juice and keeping me upright and whatnot. Oh sure, we paid taxes, we were good friends and neighbors, we had great kids, we did lots of volunteer work when I felt up to it, but we still felt, you know, hollow or something. I mean, where was all that meaning in our lives getting us? And the career of a full-time blood donor is pretty limited you know—like an athlete. That's when a miracle happened and we saw you on TV, Dirk." He sat back in his immense wicker chair.

"That's right," Dirk, the host, said softly. "You saw our little program and things have never been the same. Tell us about that."

"Well, it's true, every word of it, and whoever thinks that this is not true and that we're somehow making this up for financial gain is just plain old mean!" Mrs. McFibber said huffily, sitting forward with a huge creak of wicker.

"That's right, plain old mean," Dirk whispered contemplatively, looking toward the screen and out at us.

"And speaking of plain old mean, here's how you can

order my COMPLETE Real Estate Success System now, with operators standing by waiting expressly to take your phone call so that your life can start TODAY. Why, your old friends won't even know you or like you, you'll be so rich! Just read the books, study them even, and start making real estate offers over the phone RIGHT AWAY, offers that will be taken SERIOUSLY by some people! Isn't it exciting?"

"It sure is, Dirk," the McFibbers nodded furiously. The palm fronds swayed, the seagulls swooped, everyone's tans looked terrific.

Let's just say that you should never get out your credit card at three in the morning—not for any reason. And let's just say that if anyone needs the Complete Real Estate Success System now, I happen to have one in my basement. And let's just say that my husband does not like to talk about the time I almost was a real estate tycoon, no license and all.

CR

THE STUFF OF FAIRY TALE DREAMS

B EING A STAY-AT-HOME mom is very rewarding, and is usually fun, although at times it's no fairy tale. Giving up that extra salary is hard, and sacrifices have to be made. Our house has needed shutters around the windows since we moved in; so the house has that kind of blank, shocked look that I have in the morning without any makeup.

My husband can't take his shoes off in the traditional

show of respect when he goes to pick our teen-ager up from karate class because the heels have worn out of his work socks. He has to teeter at the threshold of the door bowing respectfully and shouting for his son to hurry up. In fact, that's how I judge the life expectancy of a sock when folding laundry—if I mutter, "He couldn't wear that to karate," then the sock is on its last leg, so to speak.

I walked my dog around town using an old belt as a leash for about a month, because her old leash was misplaced and a new leash wasn't in the budget. My husband's pants were baggy as a result, which just illuminated how old his socks were. These things have a tendency to snowball on you.

Sometimes things get even more out of hand and Mom has to get a part time job to help make ends meet. We have been there several times.

One criterion I have set, when I've had to get a part-time job, is that it has to work around my kids' schedules—and there has to be no possibility of advancement, enrichment, or fun. I've been able to satisfy all these criteria so far.

Starting the search for a good part-time job is nerve-wracking, because there are usually many varied choices.

"I've got it," I announced in a raspy voice to my husband one morning as he came downstairs for breakfast. I had been up all night watching television and thinking about my work choices.

"I saw it on a commercial. I am going to go to school at night to become a small engine aircraft mechanic," I continued, sloshing down coffee from a travel mug (just practicing) and shoving an old envelope at him, an envelope that had several movie times scrawled on it, as well as all my information to become a small engine aircraft mechanic.

"Wait a minute," he laughed, grabbing me by my coveralls (just practicing), "is this like the NETTTS opportunity that you were all hyped up about a year ago?"

"New England Tractor Trailer Training School," I said wistfully, remembering the grainy, 3 a.m. commercials that once upon a time, during another financial strain, had me hooked. "That would have worked, too, if the trucks hadn't been so darn big." My husband looked at me doubtfully.

"Honey, you can't even back down the driveway straight," he said pointedly.

"Exactly!" I shouted. "If I had gone to NETTTS I'd be able to today!"

Okay, so there's a flushed period of excitement when you are looking at your opportunities. What I really ended up doing that time, like so many other part-time workers, was retail work. Which is to say, I worked long hours for no pay and looked great doing it.

Explaining my new job to my husband was tricky; he's so into reality that it's annoying.

"Let's see now," he started, ticking off facts on his fingers as he went.

- "One: they only have 12 hours of work a week available;
- "Two: you have to *wear* their clothes, which means you have to *buy* their clothes;
- "And Three: to enable you to do this, they're giving you a fifty-percent discount on clothes."

The man looked scared.

"Yes," I nodded gleefully, "can you believe it? Think of all the money we'll save!"

Cut to three months later: I had new teenage girlfriends named Buffy and Sissy, I had three hundred clothing items on layaway for myself, I had earned ninety-three dollars net and had charged six hundred dollars on my new store credit card.

We were in debt to the store up to our eyeballs.

But on the positive side, I had never looked better. I was looking like Cinderella and living like The Old Lady Who Lived in a Shoe.

Of course, we weathered that financial storm, as well as a few since then. And once in awhile, the lure of bigger, better, and more is strong, and I have to look around carefully at the people, and not the things, to remind myself why we're sacrificing.

One afternoon, after reading our baby a fairy tale called *The Nightingale* by Hans Christian Andersen, I put him down for a nap and then dozed off on the couch and had a dream.

It must have been the fairy tale book that sparked the dream, for it went something like this:

A princess dreamed of having a beautiful nightingale of her own, to sing to her and make her happy. She pined away for a nightingale, and nothing else mattered to her except getting one. To her surprise and delight, one day one flew into her courtyard and made her life complete.

She and the nightingale were happy together, but soon she looked around and noticed that while she and her singing bird were off playing, all the other princes and princesses had built even bigger castles and had built even higher and more impressive castle walls.

So, she put the nightingale into a beautiful jewel-encrusted cage and set about building her kingdom to be even greater so that they could enjoy it together.

Her nightingale grew tired of his cage but didn't have the words to tell her, so his song became a little dimmer and a little softer.

They soon had the most beautiful castle in the land, and it was admired by all, but inside they roamed the halls separately, and inside it was quiet.

I awoke with a start and looked around. Happily-ever-after is now.

૨૪

BEING LOST

IT IS EASY to feel lost in this world. I don't mean lost in the metaphorical, philosophical sense of the word—I mean really lost. There are those of us who cannot find our way out of a paper bag when it comes to directions; in this modern world we should probably be referred to as the "geographically challenged" or the "destination impaired." Whatever you want to call us, we ain't gonna get there in time.

Now, my husband is used to this. When my husband, our first baby, and I first moved to Massachusetts from Maryland, my mom came up to visit, and we mistakenly took the Massachusetts Turnpike all the way to New York. (Is that possible?) Anyway, we took some road to New York—the point is, we weren't supposed to leave the state.

As we passed by burned out cars attended to by groups of very efficient guys relieving them of their tires, engines, and anything that would hold still, I turned to my mom, who was happily recounting some adventure or another.

"We're not in Massachusetts anymore, I don't think," which was indeed confirmed minutes later by a spotting of the Statue of Liberty.

"Let's go get some coffee and figure this out," she offered, and that's what we did. I was home in time to put the kids on the bus in the morning.

My older boys are used to problems with locations as well. "Want me to drive you guys?" I offer many times, when my teen-ager is planning a thing with his friends.

"Get your passports out," my son will mumble into his peanut butter and jelly sandwich, until I remind him that a slightly lost driver is better than no driver at all.

My husband has a compass for a brain; he could get himself from here to Peru with a good road map, toll money and some coffee. So, I often have to remind him that I process things differently. Here's him trying to get me into Boston:

"Now take Route-Blah-Blah to Exit-So-And-So . . . " until I say, "Wait! Stop being so specific! Translate it into my language!"

At this point he'll say, "Okay, okay, remember the exit we took that time you got nauseous and then you thought you saw your cousin? Turn there, and pray that the flower-cart guy hasn't moved. At him, go left. You'll see the building that you think looks like a wedding cake; it's after that."

So, I have my own ways of getting around. As long as they don't change the highways in Boston, I'll be all set.

It seems that you'll find that you're always the most lost when a) your car is full of kids, b) you're dressed up, and c) you're already late. Now, people with my directional problems depend a lot on gas station guys.

Those gas station guys can see me coming from a mile off. As I swing into the station with my window already rolled down, head hanging out, eyebrows arched in anticipation of asking for a street that doesn't exist, I roll over that hose on the cement that dings the bell, then I usually back up to get a better position and roll over it again.

The gas station attendant is usually pretty eager to help me at this point. After I ask for the street directions, I can kind of relax, because chances are I'm not going to understand the answer.

This is the time, while the attendant is gesturing and drawing in the air, that you can think about other things, like: *Gee, he has a nice face*, or *I left my watch on the back of the toilet*, or *Is that Juicy Juice running down my back?*

Then you simply thank him, roll over that hose one more time, and exit the station, turning the exact opposite way from what he told you. I've seen enough gas station attendants shaking their heads in my rear view mirror to last a lifetime.

Late last summer I was driving around with my 22-month-old, and I got lost. *No biggie*, I thought, trying to guess where I was. *We're just going to enjoy this one.*

The baby and I put on our sunglasses, turned on the radio to our station that plays hits from the '60s and '70s and kept going. As I circled around unfamiliar rotaries, we sang sympathetically to ". . . you hangin' round, baby, with Jean and Joan and who-knows-who . . ." and we took in the sights.

The baby motioned at seagulls outside his windows as we harmonized to ". . . BBBBenny and the Jets . . ."

We ate at Mi Guatemala instead of McDonald's, and we saw all sorts of people we don't see in our hometown.

Some of us need to get lost once in a while, to remember that we're living on just one tiny slice of the world. As we drove along the ocean (Atlantic? Pacific? Who knows!) birds swooped and dove as the radio played a song from the old rock group, Yes. And we honest to goodness drove into the sunset.

The song went something like this:

". . . don't surround yourself with yourself . . ."

 CR

TRIP TO THE MOON

ONE THING PARENTS need to realize about the art of child-rearing is that kids are going to eventually want to leave home. As grown-ups we need to learn to accept this idea from our kids with a grain of salt and not take it personally—even if you were in labor for days and pushed them out into the world in a burst of pain that was almost mythical in its intensity . . . but I digress.

Now this happened to me recently with both my older sons, ages 15 and 11, and it occurred just as we were getting ready to celebrate their brother's second birthday.

As we were blowing up party balloons my oldest son said to me, quite conversationally, "You do realize that when I go into the service I will probably face lots of different types of danger and I will live really far away, right?" He puffed on his little yellow balloon, supremely satisfied.

Now, I handled this exactly the way guidance counselors and top child psychologists tell you to: I shrieked, "You are doing no such thing! You're getting a nice safe job and we will always be together and that's the end of that!" Unfortunately, the mysterious static electricity that always comes with balloons was making my hair literally stand on end, so I looked like just the type of person you want to be geographically close to forever.

I thought I could count on my second son, but the same thing happened with him.

Later the same night, we were standing outside in

our front yard freezing to death because we had read that if you timed it right, you could see the space shuttle over the horizon as it carried a huge part of the space station into outer space.

"Let's locate the Big Dipper," we hissed to each other through chattering teeth while we waited.

* * *

(While we're on the subject of constellations, let's get honest, America—none of us ever really sees anything when we look up into the sky. We see a bunch of stars. I see stars that make more sense when my blood sugar is low. We all just pretend we see different constellations.

Have you ever been to a planetarium and tried your best to see Ursa Major or Cassiopeia while a passionate astronomer directed you? These folks can make a Disney adventure movie out of three stars, and we, the audience, fake it right along with him:

"Folks, assume we are straddling the meridian, with our exception being circumpolar constellations, of course," the passionate guide begins. "See Taurus the Bull glaring down on Orion? See that? Now look; Orion is leaning back on one elbow—soon he will rise up, accepting Taurus's worthy challenge. Wow, this is cool! Okay, remember your pole star and find the Big Dipper—is everyone with me?"

We all stare skywards, mouths open, necks aching, saying, "Oh, yeah!" with awe-struck gusto. In truth, the last direction we were able to follow was "No food or drinks in the planetarium, please.")

* * *

So, as I was saying, my son and I were looking up into the night sky—and he says, "I think I'm going to be one of the first humans to colonize Mars."

This one didn't even want to stay on Earth! The

nerve!

"Wait a minute, pal," I started, "we can't even locate the Big Dipper here. And I thought you were going to be a veterinarian, and I was going to be your receptionist! Let's just stick with the plan, young man!"

I discussed this mutinous behavior with my husband one night over dinner when the older boys were out.

"Why the big rush to move far away?" I asked, handing my husband a cereal bowl and a spoon. "What is it they're not getting here—oh, could you pass the Count Chocula and the milk? Thanks. Why move far away—more tap water, dear?—when we have worked so hard to provide everything they need?" We both shook our heads in puzzlement.

Soon, it was time to have the family party for the baby. As we cut the cake and sang and clapped, it seemed the baby was leaving me, too. Soon, his wispy hair would grow in and I wouldn't be able to see the outline of his head so distinctly anymore. His fingers and toes would lose their pudginess and stretch outwards, always wanting more than what was in his own yard.

As I saw everyone so clearly in the darkness of two wax candles, I made a few wishes for our baby. Bundle up when it's cold. Be kinder rather than smarter. Remember, cynicism is the cure for joy.

And if anyone ever tells you not to plant a flag on a distant battlefield or hurtle towards uncharted planets, for heaven's sake—don't listen.

CR

YARD SALE

THE REASON I love the return of spring can be summed up in two words. Now, those two words are not "blooming daffodils" or "renewed hope;" those two words are "yard sale."

The yard sale, or "tag sale" as it is known down south (or *junkae cheapae* in Latin) is one of my favorite things to attend. During Spring I can be found in the passenger seat of our car, my head swiveled around completely backwards like an owl, saying to my husband, "Pull over, darn it! I think I saw a two-handled saw back there! Look, old board games! Was that a banjo? Pull over!"

Recently, I had an opportunity to attend a huge yard sale at my middle son's school—and we kind of stumbled on it (I would have known about it if my kids ever brought notices home). My husband, our two-year-old, and I were out to run some Saturday errands, the most important of them being putting a deposit in the older boys' college funds. As we were driving along, I noticed bicycles lined up outside the school, as well as some baby equipment and furniture. A yard sale was going on!

"Pull over, pull over," I said urgently, but my husband didn't respond quickly enough so I just opened my car door and did a drop-and-roll out of the car, landing on the grass outside the school and popping right back up.

"I'm coming," I yelled to the sale, my Dr. Scholl sandals clacking as I ran through the school doors.

Most of the sale was going on in the cafeteria, and

believe me, this was a good sale. Unfortunately, it was also almost over, so I had to work quickly. At this point in the sale everything was "a buck a bag," meaning that I could fill a bag with as many items as possible and pay only one dollar for it. I shook my head, trying to make sure I heard right. Was this heaven?

I tucked bags in my waistband the way cleaning professionals do, cracked my knuckles, and I was ready. My husband came in with the baby, a worried look on his face.

"Give me the college money," I said, scanning the long tables filled with stuff.

"No—that's for the boys," my husband said, putting up his hand like a crossing guard.

"They're smart kids; they'll do just fine," I said. "Now hand it over." Do you see why we can't ever go to Las Vegas?

I settled for a five-dollar bill and a warning.

I really think sometimes I lead a charmed life; right in front of me as I walked in were two extraordinary lamps that those without vision had somehow walked right by during the sale. They were "horsie lamps," my technical appraisal jargon for two lamps whose bases were huge ceramic horse heads. I ran over to them, not believing my luck. I dragged them over to my husband, whose eyes widened.

"Here's what you do," I said, looking around suspiciously. "Don't leave these unattended. Do not go to the snack table, do not become distracted. If someone shows interest, signal me by yelling the code word 'horsie' repeatedly and we will reconnoiter right here."

I moved quickly back into the fray, targeting a table with knickknacks on it. I zeroed in on two mismatched candlesticks and was dismayed to see one of my son's teachers also closing in. We smiled, and she said something that sounded like, ". . . blah blah blah education blah blah blah," but all I could think about was those candlesticks.

Suddenly she passed right by them—I've always liked her. I put those in the bag and then proceeded to acquire other treasures like half a set of encyclopedias from 1974, a Led Zeppelin poster, a leopard-print tissue cozy, and a bent tennis racket.

When I returned to my "base camp," my husband apparently saw how hard I was working for the family, because he sat me down on a stool and kept calling me "Champ" and smearing my face with Vaseline while I spit into a bucket.

I kept shopping, but soon I was dehydrated (the horsie lamps were talking to each other), so regretfully, we paid for our stuff and left.

Back at home, the boys were sprawled out on the couch.

"Did you put our college money in the bank?" my 11-year-old asked.

"No, but we did get horsie lamps!" I answered triumphantly, my face glistening with the joy of acquisition. While my husband took most of the items right into the basement, I plugged in one of my lamps. It blinked promisingly a few times—then nothing.

Oh, well, the old saying proves true—you can lead a horsie to the Reillys', but you can't make him blink.

CR

6 ೫೦೩

WE HAVE PETS

---

*"If your husband finds himself standing outside
the supermarket on a beautiful Saturday morning
begging total strangers to 'have a heart, man, take
a kitty,' you have too many pets."*

ೞ

PET PARADE

PETS—THEY ENRICH our lives, they keep us
young, and they show us our playful side. They
also have the potential to drive us crazy, ruin our
homes, and cause spontaneous crying jags.

The key to successful pet ownership is *don't own
too many at the same time.*

- If you buy pet food in bags that weigh more than
  your own body weight, you own too many pets.
- If your husband finds himself standing outside
  the supermarket on a beautiful Saturday morning begging total strangers to "have a heart,
  man, take a kitty," you have too many pets.

- If you qualify for a small farm loan at the bank, you, as do I, probably own too many pets.

We currently are owned by three cats, one dog, and two goldfish—about six pets too many. The cats and dog were bought in that rosy time of our children's toddlerhood when we foolishly believed that these tiny people who couldn't even keep food down were going to help us care for these pets.

That's why you don't see too many teen-agers with new puppies—their parents are too smart and too broke to fall for the promises and pleadings from people who can't even vote yet. If you can't help choose a nation's leader, you shouldn't be allowed to own anything that moves and/or consumes food.

Our problem is that our pets are all aging, and frankly they're getting demanding and cranky. Their sheer number makes our house take on a circus-like atmosphere; there's always a cat hanging from a screen window, dangling from the roof, or passed out like a little drunk on the couch.

They're also getting a little too relaxed about some things if you ask me; there's nothing like hosting an intimate dinner party and shouting the highlights of your trip to Aspen over the sounds of three cats bathing themselves.

Pet owners like to talk about their pets' amazing personalities, and this is true—they are unique. But what if the personality is an offensive one? One of our cats is just plain mean—she actually taught herself to speak English so that she could yell at me when her food dish is empty.

Another has more health problems than the rest of us combined—he is currently dealing with a deviated septum and some recalcitrant post-nasal drip.

The third is just plain crazy; we like to say that he

was taken away from his mother too young. This, by the way, is what all pet owners say when their pet draws the short straw when it comes to brains.

We put up with these things and still they seem surprised to see us when we walk through "their" door each night.

Another factor in owning the cats is the litter box, or what we like to call The Issue That Divides Us. Changing the litter takes on the mental weight of choosing a retirement plan, and no one seems to be able to drag themselves down to the basement to take care of it.

The other day one of my kids called out, "Mom? There's an archaeologist at the door who has heard about the litter and wants to take some samples. Should I let him in?"

My dog is one of the larger varieties of mutt and sheds so much each day that I could actually sew another dog out of her discarded hair. I don't understand, with all this shedding, why she's not bald. I am the proud owner of fur rugs, fur furniture, and fur clothes.

My neighbor once told me that she wished that she had a faux fur to wear with an evening gown she had purchased. I invited her to come over and roll around on our family room floor before her dinner engagement, but she never showed up.

This dog is clearly my dog, so deep is her obvious devotion to me. It's actually an obsession—were she human I'm afraid we'd be looking at a stalker.

On the positive side it's not so bad to have someone so adoring at my side. She sits in the middle of the kitchen floor at night looking at the rest of the family as if to say, "Did you see that? Did you see the way she opened that can of peas? Did you notice the flair with which she defrosts? Have you ever seen it done so expertly, so well? She is amazing!"

I am actually devoted to her as well; my husband overheard me outlining my thoughts on our town's budget process to her one night and made me go lie down.

The goldfish are a recent acquisition. The choice of goldfish as pets is deceptive—sure, they only cost about a dollar a piece, until you factor in the thirty dollars a year in phone bills to the house sitter asking her to feed them while you're away.

A friend of ours recently got a new puppy, a beguiling little fellow named Tucker. It was nice to see the kinship between man and beast, and for a moment I paused; would we ever get another puppy? My husband had a good laugh, the laugh of a man who is secure in that special "over my dead body" way. I know he's right, and I was just being crazy—I was taken away from my mother too young.

CR

I DEMAND A RETRACTION FOR MY DOG

ONE OF THE simple pleasures of my life is walking my dog, Brandy. She's a large dog, half Shepherd, half Lab, and I've found that my neighbors prefer my walking her on a leash, thereby preventing her from escaping out the front door and visiting each yard— making deposits the size of my pocketbook as she strolls by.

I respond to Brandy's escapes by shrieking at the

kids and then grabbing whatever shoes are by the door—work boots, kids' sneakers, bedroom slippers and chasing her down the road, leash in hand.

One time the only shoes available were my husband's steel-tipped golf cleats, so I threw them on and click clacked down the road screaming, "Brandy! Brandy . . . right now!" The appearance was basically that of a woman in golf shoes scraping down the road screaming for a drink.

When Brandy escapes, the only sure-fire way of getting her to come back is to start the car. I don't have to actually go anywhere; I sit in the driveway running the engine, waiting for her to barrel back around the corner like the Alpo dog. My neighbors are now used to this, and know that when I'm sitting in a running car it doesn't necessarily mean I'm going anywhere.

Once in a while I do actually take Brandy for a ride around town when she returns, just so she will continue to fall for this ruse. Talk about a fool's errand. Try explaining to a policeman that you're driving with no shoes because you sometimes need to drive the dog around the neighborhood so that you can keep on tricking her. You will receive a warning and some very interesting looks.

Going on the theory that something new will spur me on to greater glory (a new shower curtain will make me clean the whole house), I recently purchased a new leash for Brandy—a retractable one. Her old nylon leash was so frayed it looked as if I was walking her with a jungle vine, so I felt the high purchase price of the new leash was justified.

The new leash looks like a little black box with a clip on the end, and Brandy was a bit skeptical when I excitedly asked, "Want to go for a walk, girl?" holding out to her what looked like a typewriter ribbon cartridge. However, she gamely jumped around when I clipped the lead to her collar, and I asked my husband if he wanted to come and try out the new leash. (We have a limited entertainment budget.)

We set off, and the leash magically lengthened as Brandy walked. My husband worked the buttons on the box to keep her a certain distance from us.

"It's like fishing," he said enthusiastically. He looked at me. "You'll need lessons."

A group of kids was approaching and I nervously said, "Reel her in."

"Right," he muttered, and found he had to run up behind her to retract to a shorter leash length. She turned and smirked at him.

We turned a corner a few minutes later and were suddenly on the outskirts of a large field, and to my horror I saw that a girls' softball game was in progress and that it was heavily attended.

Before my husband could reel Brandy in, she was winding in and out of the crowd with my husband and me hunched over like experienced wildlife trackers, desperately pushing buttons, trying to get close enough to her to send the leash back into its black box.

"Retract! Retract!" some spectators yelled helpfully as we flew by.

"We know! We know!" we screamed back, and I vowed to bring a backup leash next time.

It had all looked so easy, I despaired, remembering how I had often seen other people clipping along, holding their tiny black box with a dog dangling on the end!

"Perhaps we're just not ready for this technology," I mumbled, as we wound through the crowd, catching glimpses of Brandy's tail. We finally retracted her and stood gasping for air, bent over like winded athletes.

A few of the softball dads, having witnessed us, sauntered over to confer with my husband. They all took turns holding the leash handle, offering advice. A man can stand on a mountaintop all alone holding a screwdriver, and other men will find him, as if drawn in by a strange magnetic force, and begin to relate their own screw driving experiences.

On our way home we encountered a neighbor out in his yard, and my husband walked over to say hello. As they talked, Brandy managed to wind her new leash around both men. My husband, who could visit socially during a tornado, kept talking while pushing buttons on the leash handle as he and our neighbor were drawn closer and closer together.

"We're trying to get the hang of our new leash," I said to the neighbor, smiling, and he smiled back uncertainly, as if I'd just said we were trying to learn to eat with forks.

"I miss the old leash," my husband muttered later, as we neared home.

"It didn't do anything," I said sadly.

"Yeah, I know," he answered reflectively.

Brandy is no fool—she's thrilled. She knows it will take me a little time to learn to work my new purchase, so chances are, she'll be in the fully extended mode for some time, no fear of retraction in her near future.

Q

PRECIOUS DOG

WE ACQUIRED OUR big golden half Shepherd, half Lab dog, Brandy, back when our oldest baby was about three, and Brandy was the result of an ultimatum.

"You know," I said back then to my husband, while feeding one baby as he sat in his baby seat and carrying one baby on my hip, "I get nervous when you travel for work. I'm afraid we'll get robbed or something."

My husband looked around. Robbed? Our stereo system was an old radio alarm clock, set to an FM station, perched on the back of the couch; I was using squares of aluminum foil for placemats; and the car in the driveway was held together by duct tape.

"Anyway," I continued, "I think we should either have an alarm system installed or get a dog."

My husband said, "Huh," and walked out of the room to see what the score of the baseball game was, and I took that to mean, "Get a dog, then, if that will make you feel more secure, honey." So that's what I decided to do, now that we were both in agreement.

I really didn't know too much about dogs, so I went to the animal shelter. I showed up toting the two kids and my dreams of pet ownership. I could just see it—me walking in the woods with my dog (my kids had somehow evaporated), me sitting in front of a fire with my dog (never mind that we'd have to sit in front of the oven—we didn't have a fireplace), me a serene gray-haired woman with a dog at her feet (that would make the dog about two thousand years old in doggie years).

The lady at the shelter showed me a variety of

dogs, but seemed particularly interested in having me look at a dog that didn't seem so much Dog as it did Blur, as it jumped ecstatically in its pen.

"This is a darling puppy," she said enthusiastically.

"Umm . . . puppy?" I asked quizzically. "It looks kind of big for a puppy. How much does it weigh?"

"About seventy pounds," she said, clearing her throat.

Now, I had already shown my acumen when it comes to canines by asking her if a dog was considered a mammal, so my assuming that this gargantuan dog really was a puppy did not surprise her too much.

"Okay," I said, trying to size the dog up—it was hard to get a look at an object that moves that fast, "what's her name?"

The pound lady grabbed a leash from a hook on the wall. "Ticker," she answered. I took that as a sign.

"Oh, because she has a brave and true heart?" I asked, still trying to get a look at the dog, who was now squirming on the leash.

"Well, that and she had about a thousand ticks on her when we got her."

"No problem," I answered confidently. This train had left the station and was not coming back—I needed a dog, and this lady had one to give.

When my husband got home that night, he met Ticker. We had a spirited "discussion," and he learned that I could be impulsive, and I learned that baby elephants and baby ponies may weigh seventy pounds, but baby dogs do not.

We ended up keeping Ticker, re-named Brandy, and she became a part of the family.

Over the years she's been to every child's birthday party we've ever had. She's in almost every picture of the kids we've ever taken. She's worn bandannas and eye patches when she was called on to be a pirate, and has served as hockey goalie when the boys were a player short.

She's walked me to the bathroom during pregnancy and illness, and stayed right outside the door until I returned. She's gone without food when we've forgotten to feed her and without walks when we were too tired.

She loved the kids when they were little and smothered her with hugs, and she kept loving them when they grew older and sailed right by her, busy with their own lives.

Brandy went out to play in the last snow with the kids, and when she came inside, she lay down and had trouble getting back up again, so I took her to the veterinarian.

"She's just getting old," the vet said, gently stroking Brandy's head.

"Ah," I said back, holding tightly to her worn collar, not knowing what else to say. Suddenly I could see what my love for her had previously prevented me from seeing—her graying muzzle, her labored breathing, her eyes slightly shaded with age. She has been with us the whole time we've grown up, but we never stopped to realize that she was aging, too.

Some day Brandy will be gone, and that seems to signal the first of many changes for us as time marches on and kids grow up.

Brandy will be viewed in years to come as part of a golden time, maybe, when kids played in the street in the afternoons and whispered to each other in the dark, watched over always by their loyal dog.

I got a dog for security—little did I know just how much she would give.

"Just rest," I heard my ten-year-old say to her recently, as he sat beside her. I couldn't have said it better.

CB

7 ∞∞

OLD GLORY

"Selective worry, we call it."

∞

GRANDMA

I RECENTLY WENT "antiquing." This is a term for going to quaint little shops and paying a fortune for old furniture that has been used before.

"We already have lots of old stuff," my husband commented when I mentioned going by an antiques shop, and he's right—a young couple when starting out tends to collect a lot of old and used items. There are the fringed lampshades that children love to put on their heads and say, "hello, dah-ling," when playing dress-up. There's the old wooden ladder in the garage that once broke when two birds landed on it at once. There are my prized gargoyle teacups and my coffee table that weighs as much as our car.

So, he had a point.

On this particular jaunt, I realized that shopping for antiques kind of makes me uncomfortable, first because you are expected to haggle over price. I am not a haggler; I'd much rather pay any kind of full price and toddle away happily with my purchase.

My husband is a haggler—he once haggled at Sears. Sears doesn't haggle. We went to Sears to get a new washing machine and it was one salesman's unhappy day. My husband strode up to the washing machine I liked and said, "We like this washing machine, sir. I'll give you fifty bucks for it. Do we have a deal?"

The salesman looked a little taken aback. Rolling a toothpick around in his mouth, he said, "This is Sears. We don't bargain here. The ticketed price is final, I'm afraid."

My husband shook his head regretfully in the classic bargainer's way and said, "Okay, I'll give you fifty-seven bucks for it. You're killing me, here. Do we have a deal?"

Needless to say, we left Sears and bought a washer somewhere else at full price and even purchased the extended warranty (which covers anything wrong with the washing machine that does not involve water or the washing of clothes).

So, I am a little apprehensive about buying antiques. Also, they are definitely not in our budget, and I know only one thing about antiques: they're old. That is where my knowledge ends. You might as well send me out to buy parts for the Hubble telescope. But, I was willing to give antiquing a whirl.

Recently, I stopped by an antique shop that was more like an antique barn, loaded with furniture, cracked mirrors, and dusty knick-knacks. I looked around.

"Jeepers," I said aloud to myself, "everything here

is so old." The lady running the antiques barn heard this intelligent comment and was over like a shot.

"Can I help you?" she asked.

"Yeah, I thought I might buy an antique or two," I answered, looking around.

"What style are you interested in?" she asked pleasantly. Here I was going to have to wing it.

"Well, kind of a Shaker, Mediterranean, French-Revivalist thing, with kind of an Early-American art-deco influence thrown in," I answered, gazing around me. I was seeing a lot of dressers with knobs missing and a lot of old pictures of brave, billowy ships on stormy seas. I turned back to the lady. "Got anything like that?"

She suddenly remembered some paperwork, and I was on my own again. As I walked around I overheard a young couple talking as they studied a tiny cabinet so hard that they were breaking a sweat. One said, "Maybe this would go well in the upper hallway—you know, under the lithograph, where the light filters in around four o'clock. Kind of an *Out of Africa* feel, you know?"

I tried to imagine the same conversation between my husband and me over the little cabinet—"Well, maybe we could cram this in between the vacuum cleaner and the refrigerator where the cat goes to cough up fur balls. Kind of a *Psycho* feel, you know?"

I ended up coming home with an old checkerboard which was purchased without haggling. I'm getting my feet wet, so to speak, when it comes to antiques (although I have a dining room set on hold back at the barn).

Relaxing over a cup of tea served in my trusty gargoyle teacup, I thought about my favorite antiques, which have no monetary value at all. They are some hatpins that belonged to my grandmother who passed away years ago, and they are in a baggie tucked away in a drawer.

When I look at them, I can feel her personality rush back to me. I remember the grandmother who took as serious business a child's request to "just lay down with me for a minute." I remember the woman who, I now know, never had much in terms of money, but who always had a house filled with visiting relatives and doting friends. I remember a woman who got such pleasure over a good ice cream soda and yet was exceedingly refined. About the time hatpins were in vogue she had one son serving as a fighter pilot in World War II, another son in high school, and a baby girl, my mother, in her arms. Oscillating fans, piano-playing heard faintly on a summer's walk, and tomatoes on the vine remind me of her.

I wouldn't take anything for these hatpins—a good antique, when pulled out of a drawer and looked at with a friend, makes your eyes fill with tears as you say, "I just wish you could have known her."

CR

THE BASEMENT

L AST WEEKEND I cleaned our basement. This is one of the most unrewarding areas to clean—first of all, no one sees it even when it is clean. Of course, you could try to get people down there—a friend stopped by to chat, and when she asked to use the bathroom, I said, "Sure! Oh, just one thing—if you like to use toilet paper I have some down in the basement." So, she did ooh and aah over it right before she sprinted upstairs.

This recent basement cleaning came about because our furnace started making its annual funny noises when we turned the heat on for the cooler season.

My whole family sat poised at the dinner table, forks suspended over their plates, eyes looking far away in concentration as the furnace started banging and clang-ing—it sounded as if a mess hall cook was down there whipping up grub for the troops. (Actually, wouldn't it be great if there were—I could just send the family down-stairs at dinnertime with a paper plate and a tin cup.)

My husband sighed and said dejectedly, "We are living on borrowed time with that thing. We're going to have to have the furnace guy come over and give us an estimate."

Now, my first thought was not about the expense of a new furnace or the inconvenience of hauling the old one out . . . it was about the furnace man having to see the basement! The basement is a family secret! As far as everyone knows, we're normal!

"Oh, good grief," I said quickly, "we're going to have to clean it up a little."

The kids burst out laughing. A little? We've sent repair people down there that we're still looking for to this day. I don't even actually go down there any more; I just open the door and chuck things down, using the proven homemaker's strategy of, "I'll deal with it later."

As luck would have it, the next day the older kids had activities that started very early, so they were out of the house by dawn. My husband and I stared at each other warily over coffee.

"So," he started out casually, "I think the baby misses me. I think I'll spend some good ol' quality time with him today." The baby answered his prayers and smiled at him encouragingly.

"Oh, okay," I mumbled. "I'll straighten up the basement." Who can fight a smiling baby?

The first thing I did was to grab my teen-ager's boom box—for all I knew there was electricity down in the basement and I could listen to music as I worked.

The second thing I did was to have a good cry.

The third thing I did was to open the basement door, encountering the steps leading downstairs, which I like to call "Fur Alley." These steps are where I put the dog when she starts barking at people who ring the doorbell, and the fur from these stairs sucks onto your clothes the minute you open the basement door.

I came up to answer the telephone a few minutes after being on the stairs, and it looked as if Chewbacca from *Star Wars* was on our phone confirming a dentist's appointment.

The baby started crying when he saw me—"mama gone," he kept saying. I lumbered back downstairs.

The next task was to try to enter the basement. Laundry, boots, towels, tools, paper bags, plastic bags, inflatable pools, small farm equipment and such were directly impeding my progress to the basement itself.

I started working away, tossing these back up the stairs where they lay covered in fur for proper assorting later. It looked like an episode of *Lassie* where Timmy is caught in a collapsed mine shaft and his mom is working feverishly in her housedress to get him out using nothing but a can opener and a dishtowel.

Finally, I broke through the mess and tumbled into the actual basement itself.

"Whoa," I said in wonder, brushing myself off and looking around. Stalactites hung from the ceiling, stalagmites and steam rose from the ground, and hidden treasures abounded—why, my wedding album was down there! I sat right down to look at it, but was soon battling wildly-tearing eyes, a runny nose, hives, and Teletubbies apparitions.

I struggled to find the source of my discomfort and grabbed onto a plastic sword jammed into a box for protection as I stalked around, a furry, dusty Chewbacca carrying a plastic sword and a wedding album.

"Aha!" I yelled, both triumphant and aghast at the same time: the cat litter—if that's what you could call it at this point. I put down my sword and considered— I know I got out of changing it when I was pregnant with the baby, and he's almost two, now, so . . . oh, well, sometimes it's better not to dwell on unpleasantness. We would just hope that traveling research scientists would happen along soon and take it away.

Once I started working, it went pretty fast. I located the washer and dryer, stacked boxes, and swept the floor. By the time my husband came down with some coffee, I was actually decorating the basement, perhaps a little light-headed from the cat litter fumes.

"This looks great," he said enthusiastically, swiping fur off my back and looking around. It was nice to have the job appreciated, and I had to agree.

No Wookiee could have done better.

CR

DO-IT-YOURSELF

I DON'T NECESSARILY like to give advice—usually those most willing to give advice are those most unwilling to take it.

But in the instance where I find myself right now, I'm going to go ahead and give some advice: if you want to stay married to your husband or wife, don't re-do a house together—in fact, run screaming from any house you may be considering buying that needs substantial work before it comes anywhere close to looking attractive.

If you are considering purchasing a home and find yourself saying any of the following . . .

- "I've always thought outhouses were rather charming,"
- "The locals say Paul Revere may have slept here," or,
- "I bet we can work on the house at night and on weekends—the kids will help!"

. . . walk quickly to your car, get in, and drive far, far away from that bad place. You'll thank me later.

My husband and I have decided to fix up our kitchen. Our home is about seventy years old, and it is full of its own special history. We think that the kitchen is the actual location where they used to film the old war movies where the soldiers would hunker down in the trenches while bombs exploded around them.

The last painting of the kitchen coincides with the first Apollo space flight—apparently that worthy craft actually blasted off from our actual kitchen, as remarkable as that sounds—it's really the only way to explain the craters and cracks in our kitchen ceiling.

All of this history has worn out the old kitchen. When you're in the kitchen standing at the sink and it rains on your head whenever others shower, you've got problems. But we ignore this—a repair of the plumbing is going to cost a fortune, so why even worry about it? Selective worry, we call it.

Instead, we're going to paint the kitchen and replace the floor—basically because I had what we quietly refer to as "the incident"—I completely lost my mind while making breakfast one morning.

As my family was innocently eating breakfast, I wheeled around from the stove and yelled, "I cannot work in this kitchen one more minute! I take pride in my work here at home! (They were eating stale doughnuts and drinking water.) I am an artist and this kitchen is my palette! We are going to start the work as soon as possible, if not sooner, bubs!"

Needless to say, they all looked as if a scary alien had landed right in the middle of the kitchen—but they knew I meant business, so the kids, being the helpers that they are, rushed to the phone and made plans with their friends for the next two weeks straight.

My husband looked at me. "What's wrong with the kitchen, honey?" he asked as a piece of the ceiling fell onto his plate. He got up and slid down the floor over to me (the floor is severely slanted). "But we'll re-do it, if it makes you happy."

We started out strong.

"This is going to look great," we said enthusiastically to each other, flushed with the thought of a kitchen that we could be proud of (right now the colors of the kitchen are blue and black—like a bruise).

"I'll put some dried flowers over there, and maybe

hang some decorative kitchen implements from colonial days," I mused aloud happily, as my husband tried to work some life into an old paintbrush we must have forgotten to clean after our last massive home improvement job. Bending wrought iron would have been easier.

"Well, I need to go to the paint store and spend hundreds of dollars on supplies that I already have but just can't find," he sighed, leaving.

When he came back I was happy to report that I had cleaned out the sink and looked at about two hundred old photos I had found in one of the kitchen drawers—and we were ready to breathe life into our vision.

We spread out the newspaper, arranged our sandpaper, screwdrivers, and paintbrushes, and talked about moving again rather than start this project.

We also tried to convince ourselves that the kitchen isn't really that out-of-date, but the meat grinder on the wall, the butter churn in the corner, and the rotary dial on our kitchen telephone told a different story. We will officially begin the project this week—we decided to go out to dinner and review our kitchen makeover strategy, so no actual work has been done.

We're kind of dreading starting; we like being married. My husband has a little bit of a tendency towards, oh, shall we say, "bossiness," when it comes to home improvement. So, we'll see how it goes, but I am ready to work.

And I'm looking forward to seeing more old photos!

CR

MY GREEN THUMB
ALWAYS TURNS BROWN

NO MATTER WHICH way I look at it, I am just not a gardener. Each spring, as I drive by people loading their cars with flats of flowers, small shrubs, and even little trees, I gaze at them with the admiration and envy I have for astronauts and cellular biologists.

I start out strong. Each season I dutifully buy a pair of gardening gloves (which also make good oven mitts and can substitute as winter gloves, if needed), and two or three packages of seeds that will move around in my junk drawer for years to come.

I then go to one of the local gardening centers, which more often than not also has a gift shop. You can buy not only flowers, but herb teas, quilts, or a couch, if you need one. (Do they have many customers that come in for a begonia and leave with an ottoman?)

I don't know plant names, so I then have a disjointed, nerve-wracking conversation with a nursery worker that consists of me pantomiming the plant I want and the worker feverishly guessing the answer.

"It has little cone-shaped thingies growing out of a stalk-like stem—very delicate, and gives the appearance of floating, if you see it from the road," I say, drawing in the air.

The nursery worker then guesses until he hits on the plant or retires, whichever comes first. I always leave with geraniums.

My husband and I are mulchers at heart. Bald spot on the lawn? Mulch it. A pile of last winter's Christmas wreaths stacked by the porch? Mulch it. Kids running by being annoying? Mulch them, too.

There are never too many spots that a little mulch couldn't help. From an airplane, my lawn looks like a leopard.

Possibly the biggest thing about mulch, though, is that my husband gets to go get it in our truck. He even goes to order it in the truck, hauling back one small receipt. No matter how small the job, if it has to do with the house or the yard, we use the truck.

We may own a parcel of land the size of a postage stamp and wouldn't know how to bale hay even if you threatened to take away our ATM cards; but make no mistake, we are going to Home Depot in the truck if it kills us.

We are motivated to garden by upcoming events at our house where people will have to see our yard (we've found that people cannot be trusted to put on blindfolds at the corner of our street even if they promise to). When we bought our current house, I was thrilled to see things already in bloom that I could take credit for when visitors came.

Two weeks ago we were planning a party for our youngest son's first communion. As my husband and I were standing around in the backyard, I mentioned that we had to fix up the yard.

"What?" my husband grunted, trying to pry the lid of the gas grill open—we forgot to put a cover on it over the winter. "The yard just needs to be raked, that's all."

Raked? Rearranging deck chairs on the Titanic ring a bell? As I fought my way over to the corner of the yard, shielding my face from low-hanging branches, my husband chuckled.

"You look like Sigourney Weaver in that jungle

movie," he commented, sidling along the side of the house in an attempt to reach the garage. (I pictured myself greeting our guests at the door with a hug, wearing a pair of mud boots and a mosquito helmet.)

My husband made it to the garage, where he stared inside, half curious, half afraid. "I think I see the lawn chairs!" he shouted triumphantly.

Those were left out in the elements last year, too. Our guests would be visiting politely, balancing food on their laps, bent over almost double at the waist should we set out these rust-hinged spectacles.

We had work to do! I picked out a section of ground and started weeding. I pulled and grunted.

My kids ran by amused. "What are you doing, Mom?" they asked.

"Gardening," I answered, and a moment later turned to see their retreating forms growing smaller and smaller as they fled. It's amazing how fast they can move when confronted with manual labor.

A neighbor heard me and came over. I proudly showed her my weeding work.

"Oh, you didn't want those tulips there?" she asked. I looked at my husband with a face that said: *moving again to a new neighborhood wouldn't be that hard.*

I'm trying to be philosophical about my lack of gardening talent. This yard has a lot to teach me, I'll just bet. And I'm going to learn.

I'm a little nervous, though. My husband mentioned that he was going to buy a broadcaster, whatever that is. I find myself hoping it's a man who will stand in my living room and bring me news, sports and weather every half hour.

CR

CIRCUS BEDROOM

HAVE YOU EVER watched a program on television that was so darn depressing that it took you a while to recover from it?

Now, I'm not talking *ER* here, or *NYPD Blue* even—I'm talking about another group of initials that will depress the daylights out of you: HGTV.

HGTV is House and Garden Television and is a 24-hour cable channel. There, at any hour of the day or night, you can find someone with gobs of money (which you won't have) and gobs of expertise (which you won't have) ready to show you how to make your house or garden beautiful.

A few weeks back I was flipping around and I happened to stumble on HGTV. A very stylish woman was wafting through a beautiful chiffon-adorned bedroom and talking to the camera in wistful, sighing tones.

"Have you ever," she began, running a perfectly manicured nail around an ornate bedpost, "looked around and said, 'Well, hey, I wish my bedroom were more romantic, and yet more functional at the same time'? Have you ever done that?"

I looked around: I was slumped on an unmade bed, next to a stack of dirty dishes, and a dog was scratching herself half-heartedly at my feet. Functional romance? Sure, I was up for that.

If I had to choose one word to describe my bedroom, that word would be "circus." And it's not just the trapeze and popcorn vendor that makes me say that. We literally do not sleep, it's so crazy in there.

The first problem we run into, when my husband

and I finally shut off the lights and try to fall into our separate comas, is one of our cats, who invariably comes to the window as soon as we have reached REM sleep. (I think I've actually seen the cat out there with a little stopwatch, muttering to himself, "They should be just about asleep by now; I'll begin.") This cat starts scratching the windowpane, and I don't mean a little tentative scratching. I mean "dig-a-tunnel-to-China" scratching.

Why do cats do this? Do they think that they are somehow superior to glass—do they think that they have a prayer of actually scratching through to the indoors?

My husband bolts out of bed in his underwear, hair standing on end, and always says the same thing as he wrestles with the old window: he says, "I don't believe it."

Why doesn't he believe it? It happens every night.

The next section of the night I like to think of as The Futile Climb to Nowhere. As my husband and I desperately try to sleep, we are slowly, almost imperceptibly, sliding down to the end of the bed. I believe that this happens because one of the corners of our bed is supported by phone books, due to the fact that my oldest son broke the bed when he and eight close friends jumped on it during his eleventh birthday party.

So, instead of replacing the frame like normal people, we propped it up with a few old college textbooks and phone books. It still is not quite even; we'll need to move to a bigger town with a larger phone book population to get the kind of height we need. So, we inch up the bed all night long, grunting as we try to stay asleep while climbing.

We might as well not bother—when we get to the top we will just be greeted by our extremely flat pillows. We cannot figure out why the heck our pillows are always so flat.

"Buy quality pillows," our friends and family have advised us, as we listen gratefully while rotating our heads painfully back into the forward position.

So, we take their advice, and we always start out with such high hopes; I come back from the store with two huge, new fluffy pillows, and my husband and I smile knowingly.

This is gonna be it! our looks say. *These bad boys will stay puffed up forever.*

Alas, we're always disappointed; they deflate like a tire with a nail stuck in it. I have come to the conclusion that our heads are too heavy. We're not quite sure what to do with that information.

We end the middle portion of the night listening to our old dog have dreams and nightmares while she's sleeping at our feet. As her toenails scrape the floor and she yips, yelps, yaps and twitches, my husband rolls over.

"This is useless," he mumbles miserably. "I have to get up in one hour, at which time I will be absolutely dead to the world. I should just get up now."

I just sigh, stacking up the wafer-thin pillows under my incredibly heavy head.

Soon, my husband's alarm clock goes off. My husband had this alarm clock in college, and it's seen better days. It is encased in dust that I can't get off it, and it is so static-y that when the radio comes on in the morning it sounds like an alien from another planet is trying to make contact with us via ham radio.

So, our day begins. After listening to the lady on HGTV, I'm convinced that all this, plus world peace, could be resolved with a few aromatherapy candles and a really upbeat attitude. Of course, she would say things like that. She seemed to have a really light head.

CR

8 ⟨೩⟩೩

VACATION DAYS

"Red Alert. Suburban woman in red canoe
approaching — wearing a Cape Cod sweatshirt,
dangling question-mark earrings, and wedgie
sandals. Danger — pass it on."

೩

CARNIVAL COMES TO TOWN

MY KIDS WERE thrilled recently by a special occasion in the neighborhood—the traveling carnival came to town. Kids will behave for minutes on end if they hear that the carnival is coming; it's a documented fact.

This little carnival comes to our town every year, and it happens to set up tent (literally) right at the bottom of our street. A neighbor of ours, back when he had just moved into his home and didn't know about the carnival, was proudly surveying his new yard one day and was startled to look up just in time to see a giraffe walk by. Needless to say, he stayed out of the sun for the rest of the day.

This year my husband and I, along with our ten-year-old, pushed our new baby down to the carnival to check it out and to check out the whereabouts of our oldest son, now a teen-ager. As soon as he spotted us he ran over, eyes glazed, sweat glistening on his face, and, never making direct eye contact with us, thrust his hand out and mumbled something that sounded like "Money. Need some. Now." Then he was off again, under cover of darkness.

We started looking around, and it was a spectacle—grown-ups spending their weekly paychecks trying to win a two-dollar stuffed animal, whole faces lost in clouds of cotton-candy, reams of tickets spilling like sausage links out of kids' pockets.

"Look, fried dough," I cried, pointing to a booth nearby.

"We'll stop by there on the way home," my husband said happily. Rock concerts used to make us this happy; now all it takes is fried dough.

The number of rides at this carnival was pretty amazing, but it occurred to me as I looked around that they looked kind of—how you say—rickety.

At home I trail around after my kids holding out dental floss, I make them eat fruit a couple of times a year, they've never missed an immunization, and yet I freely, without a thought, let them board rides that shoot them into outer space and look as if they're held together with grease and chewing gum. I saw my teen-ager whip by on the Scrambler, his head cracking into another boy's head, both of them howling with delight.

We got into line with other hot, sweaty carnival-goers. My ten-year-old looked up at me.

"Hey, Mom," he said, "want to go on the Tilt-A-

Whirl with me?"

I was all ready to tell him that I'd rather use cou-
pons or go back to my natural hair color than go on
one of these scary rides—when I heard a sound . . .
my husband's quiet snort of amusement at our son's
innocent question. *Okay,* I thought huffily, *so I had
hallucinations on the Ferris wheel at Canobie Lake.
And maybe I did make a line two miles long back up so
I could be excused from riding the roller coaster at Six
Flags—big deal!*

"Sure," I said, taking his hand. "Dad will watch the
baby."

We inched closer and closer to the Tilt-A-Whirl,
and the fellow running the ride became the most important person on the planet to me.

"So," I said casually to him as we waited, "every-
thing going all right for you tonight? Feeling good?
Marriage going okay? Were you a fan of Foghat's *Slow
Ride?*" He was a little annoyed, it's safe to say.

Finally, it was our turn. My son, a friend of his,
and I all boarded the ride.

"Where are the seatbelts for the kids?" I muttered,
and was given a look that had "nerd" written all over
it. "Okay," I said enthusiastically, "let's start 'er up!" I
waved to my friend who was running the ride, and was
pleased to see that he saw me. "He'll take extra good
care of us, kids!" I confided to the boys.

"Hey, did you see the kid that barfed as soon as he
got off this?" my son's friend said to my son conversationally, as the ride started up with a wheeze and a
bang. "I thought he was gonna die!" This was the last
thing I heard before our descent into the nether
reaches.

The Tilt-A-Whirl basically tilts and whirls at very
high speeds, and during the ride—that must have

lasted five hours—our little car seemed to be tilting and whirling much faster than all the others. The kids squealed in delight while I was presented with the before-death montage of scenes from my life that I've heard is common before dying.

When the ride finally, mercifully stopped, the kids yelled, "Cool!" and disembarked, while I stooped to look for my contact lenses that had flown out of my eyeballs when the ride got going.

"Honey, you're green!" my husband said, strolling the baby up to meet me.

I waved weakly to the ride operator, who I'm sure felt sorry that he wasn't just the teensy-weensiest bit more alert during the ride.

"I will never eat again," I said to my husband, our faces aglow in a neon haze.

"Not even fried dough?" he asked.

"After the fried dough, never will I eat again," I said.

And off we went.

ଔ

COKE WARDEN

I AM GETTING over the week-long school vacation of my sons, ages ten and 14.

I am able once again to see the cushions on my couch—there aren't any kids lounging on them.

Our baby can once again nap in peace—there aren't any kids crashing up and down the stairs.

A liter bottle of Coke can actually survive more than an hour on the kitchen counter—my kids like to start their inhalation of Coke by washing down their daily multivitamin with a big glass of it during vacation week. I become, during their vacations, the Coke Warden—all I seem to say is, "How much soda have you had? Don't go get any soda, now. Tell your friends, no soda!"

Kids tend to rebel against any type of instruction during their time off.

"Would you please pick that gum wrapper up off the floor?" I asked my 14-year-old during vacation week as I staggered by him, carrying the baby in one arm, cleaning supplies in the other, and balancing a load of towels on my head like Carmen Miranda. I had just cleaned up a pet accident.

My son looked at me from his comfortable position on the couch, where he had been lying since the huge exertion of leaving his bed, and then looked at the gum wrapper, which, being just a gum wrapper, was about the size of a gnat.

"Oh," he groaned, "can't you get it? I am wicked tired, Mom." He was punished for this by not being allowed to have Coke for the next 15 minutes.

My kids like to use the week off to play outside, which is fine with me. The thing is, I have boys and they like to play Army, and over the years they have collected an impressive array of army paraphernalia: jackets, boots, backpacks, and toy weapons.

When they were little and I was part of their play, they even included me—(sometimes when I'm feeling a little nostalgic I put on my camouflage bathrobe I got one Mother's Day and dart around the house, looking furtive).

So, on Vacation Week my house turns into Fort Reilly—a fort that would shame any real army. (Fort Reilly watches *Later Today* and serves Fluffernutter for lunch.)

I will be reading the paper or filing my nails when seven or eight "army men" pop up, dressed in camouflage and looking pretty non-military as they wander around the kitchen, no doubt looking for Coke to pilfer.

"I'm thinking about taking a college course, maybe in the Social Sciences or perhaps something on the History of Human Thought," I'll say loftily to a friend on the phone, as army commandos rappel off the sides of the house and jump from the roof. *Who am I kidding?* I ask myself, hiding the Coke.

Kids tend to run out of steam by mid-week of Vacation Week.

"We're bored," both boys whined at me from where they were lying on the floor, tossing a rubber ball back and forth to each other.

"Well," I answered enthusiastically, "I thought maybe we could go down to Boston and walk the Freedom Trail, maybe follow Paul Revere's midnight ride."

"Or we could walk down to Burger King and Supersize some fries," they answered, reaching for their jackets.

By the end of the week, as the kids' boredom increased, I took to disappearing.

"Mom," one of the kids yelled impatiently, as I hid in the bathroom with the baby, reading a magazine, "which one of us knows the lyrics to 'N Sync better, me or him?" (It's best to ignore these types of inquiries.)

Finally, the week drew to a close. All the Coke was drunk, the army gear lay in a neglected heap on the floor, and I was muttering to myself in foreign languages (I actually don't speak any).

On Sunday night, just when I was starting to relax, homework was remembered.

"You've had all week to do this!" I shrieked, sorting through rulers, calculators and scraps of paper to try to get a look at the assignments.

"Yeah, but we were too busy," answered the kids who had almost died of boredom.

On Monday, alone in the house again, I took stock. We never made it to a museum, or walked the Freedom Trail, or went to the Science Center. And I had that almost wistful feeling of missing the boys, even though it was so chaotic when they were around full-time.

"Oh well," I said to the baby, "soon we'll have the pleasure of their company all summer."

He said "goo-goo" in agreement, and off we went, to go get a Coke together.

CR

THE OLD SWIMMING HOLE

IT'S SUMMERTIME, WHICH means it's time to make my annual pilgrimage to my hometown in Maryland, and to visit with my family there.

Leaving my husband behind, this year I made the summer journey down south with my three boys. It would be fair to say that on these visits I regress a little—I was wearing bunny slippers, eating peanut butter and jelly sandwiches, and braiding my sister's hair by the end of Day One of the ancestral-home visit.

One thing I forgot, though, about taking off the rose-colored glasses of adulthood. Being a kid wasn't all bunny slippers and hair-braiding. Some of it was dealing with things like frequenting the town swimming pool.

Using a town swimming pool is an interesting experience when you're an adult; for one thing, you're a lot bigger. Jumping into the shallow end for the first time in 15 years, I almost broke both my legs in half, seeing as I am about three feet taller than when I last used the old neighborhood pool.

This difference in height caused me to hit the bottom of the pool and shoot up out of the water like a show-offy synchronized swimmer. My kids, watching at the time, swam quickly away muttering, "Well, she didn't have many friends growing up if she did things like that!"

It was about 100 degrees out the day we chose to use this town pool, so it was crowded. Hyper, wet kids of all sizes, shapes, and colors quickly surrounded me. Adults stood waist deep discussing politics and current events while little kids banged into them under water, turning their thighs purple and blue, sputtering to the top and gasping, "Sorry!" and spewing different bodily fluids before submerging again.

I decided to use the diving board—something I haven't done in years. Let's just say that a lot of things were shaking now that weren't shaking then, as I bounced on the board above the diving well. Slowly, without meaning to, while trying to decide whether to do a cannonball or just jump in, I was becoming one of those obnoxious swimmers who bounce for hours in preparation for their dive.

Swimmers stopped and turned to watch my much-anticipated dive; my own children were in awe—might I have a physical talent after all?

"Mom, the lifeguard wants you to stop hogging the board," one of my kids said nervously.

"Well, he's not the boss of me," I answered back, caught in a vicious cycle of bouncing (when I'm under pressure my speech patterns start to slide).

When the board finally stopped reverberating under my feet, I sort of fell into the water, hands pointed out in front of me, body curled in a slumping position similar to a sack of potatoes when it's thrown from the back of a truck. I'm sure Greg Louganis, wherever he was, breathed a sigh of relief

Another universal thing about using municipal facilities is the baby pool, or "big, outdoor potty." I wandered over to the baby pool and saw toddlers and babies playing happily while pee-peeing at astonishing rates into the water. No plants grow around baby pools, you'll notice, and the mommies and daddies sound like a bunch of Darth Vaders breathing through their mouths to avoid the telltale smells that waft skyward.

I put my foot into the baby pool water and my toenail polish fell off my toes and my foot shriveled up to about the size of a walnut. A little toothless person grinned up at me from the depths of her Hercules raft, Teletubby swimmers, and Barney life vest—she needed all that because her diaper had exploded to the size of a beach ball and must have had a water-weight of about 30 pounds.

This is not to say that worries about "accidents" are confined to the baby pool. Back when I was a kid, the lifeguards let it be known that super-secret NASA scientists (probably the NASA professionals that opt to study pee in town pools rather than boring old space travel) had come up with a red dye that, when released into the pool water, would be activated by urine and would follow around anyone who was tempted to use the pool as their own personal bathroom.

Back then I had looked at my friends doubtfully— we knew some little kids who would become human Etch-A-Sketches should this dye thing be real. I never saw the red dye personally—but suddenly bathroom lines got a lot longer.

My kids and I enjoyed our time at the town pool— the kids relaxed and drank expired sodas (the soda machines were kind of forgotten at the close of the season) and watched me swim crooked laps in the lap lane.

We showed up back at my parents' doorstep with bloodshot eyes, clogged ears, and at least one of us had sore, aching muscles.

On the up side—I'm thinking, just thinking, of signing up for diving lessons when we get home.

‹♦›

KIDS' VACATION

I AM GEARING up for summer, which of course means gearing up for the fact that my kids will be out of school for two and a half months.

My town has three separate yearly school vacation weeks, beginning in December, and I've barely just gotten over them. Far be it from me, but I say the more time our kids are hunched over a microscope or learning about Mayan civilizations, the better.

At the beginning of each of these three separate vacations I am in my best motherly form, perkily looking through newspapers with dreams of museums, plays, and well-planned spontaneous talks about the meaning of life dancing through my head.

At the end of each of these weeks, I am always led, drooling, up to the bedroom where I am given a nice snack and some construction paper and urged to "make something real pretty."

My kids are very social, and I am grateful that they have so many friends. But after driving them and their friends around for a week, picking up and dropping off various assortments of kids in baggy clothes, I am a little less grateful for their sociability.

On one trip I was chauffeuring a kid I didn't even recognize, and asked, "Do we know you?"

"It's cool," he answered languidly, putting his headphones back on, rocking back and forth to his music so hard I think he was affecting my gas mileage.

I visit the ATM 324 times during vacation week and always pray that they will start loading these machines with cookies as well as cash, so I can grab some nutrition while we're on the road.

I become friends with the drive-thru lady at McDonald's—when I start to order, craning my head out the window and shouting in the general direction of the speaker she squawks back, "Deirdre? Is it you? Have you been home since your last order?"

"No," I answer sadly, becoming teary at the memories of my house and driveway.

We invariably go to the movie matinee at some point during the week, where my kids distance themselves from me as much as humanly possible. It's amazing how the same creatures that begged me for rides, money, and candy stare at me quizzically, as if trying to place my face the minute we're inside the theater complex.

On one such trip I made the mistake of yelling out, "Do you have your ticket stub, sweetpea?" to my oldest child (a preteen), and the whole theater froze. Popcorn stopped popping, cash registers were silent, other moms and dads looked away sorrowfully, feeling my pain and yet happy it was not they who had lapsed, they who had forgotten the code.

I answer so many questions on vacation that I hunger for silence and look forward to a trip to the bathroom. Questions such as "Why do I have eyebrows?" and "Does soccer make everyone grumpy, or is it just me?" defy answering.

Of course I am not in this alone. Other parents are going through the same thing and are desperate to talk, to have adult contact. I have stayed on the phone for hours just to talk to a friend, knowing full well that the house will be wrecked and vast projects involving pillows, blankets, all our pets, and probably food will have been started.

So now, here comes summer, just when I've recuperated from April vacation. All I talk about now is "summer programs." My friends and I confer about what programs we're going to put our kids into with the same zeal we used to plan our nights out with each other.

I will stand in line from the crack of dawn for hours with no coffee just to sign my kids up for an activity that will take up about ten hours of each week total this summer.

I have seen parents weep when told at the registration desk that a program is closed.

I didn't save the receipt when I ordered a bedroom set, but I framed the receipt from summer program sign-ups. There is no way my kids will not be on that basketball court this summer, with some other adult (preferably one with a whistle) entertaining them.

Still, I am lucky to be home with them. At the end of both summer and vacation week I take pleasure in knowing that they have had a good time and have gotten a break to be just kids. It is worth it.

Although once, my husband had the poor timing to ask me, right after vacation week, if I thought we'd ever have another baby.

I think my maniacal laughter as I pulled out of the driveway probably answered his question.

CR

UP, UP AND AWAY

RECENTLY, I TOOK a quick trip home to Maryland to introduce my 16-month-old baby to his great-grandmother, who was up visiting Maryland from Florida. Since it was a quick trip, and since I wasn't keen on spending 18 million hours in the car with a baby, we flew. I haven't flown an awful lot in the last few years—our extra money in the bank has "emergency furnace replacement" written all over it. But fares are pretty low these days, so the baby and I were taking a trip.

Right off the bat, as soon as we reached the ticket counter, paperwork was involved. I needed a birth certificate to prove that our baby is, in fact, a baby. The drooling, babbling, and being a little short on hair apparently were not enough evidence of this.

Security is also tighter in airports these days—there was a poster of a gun and a bomb with big "Xs" through them and the caption, "We Take All Comments Seriously!"

Now, I am the type that the minute you tell me definitely not to say something, I am doomed to say it. Sweat was rolling down my face as I smiled blankly at the ticket agent and used all the forces of my will not to say, "I'm going to visit my parents, Mr. and Mrs. Bomb. We will be going to see *Annie Get Your Gun.*"

Also, there is a little quiz on whether you packed your bags yourself and are you the only one who has been in contact with them. Who hadn't been in my bags is more like it—one kid relieved me of my hair products, another thought he saw the outline of a pack of gum in a side pocket, and my husband snuck a pair of his boxer shorts from my bag back into his drawer

(Okay—I didn't have time to do my laundry; that's how it goes).

After the ticket counter, we all proceeded to the gate. Now, this gate will always be about exactly thirty miles from the ticket counter if you are traveling with small children or anyone in need of assistance.

As my husband, kids and I struggled along carrying a baby, two baby bags, a car seat and a stroller, those important-sounding airport vehicles kept buzzing by us, cute little lights strobing, little warning sounds bleeping as they rushed by carrying no one at all. Why are these vehicles always empty? What do you have to do—what condition do you have to be in—to merit one? If they will drive by a family gasping for oxygen and staggering under the weight of their baby paraphernalia, the bar must be pretty high.

Next, we arrived at the gate, and I was issued a boarding pass the size of a restaurant menu. Soon after, it was time to say good-bye to the family. My older kids were pretty choked up; they had to hide their feelings by running directly to the gift shop and browsing through all the sweatshirts, hats, and toys for sale.

Soon, the baby and I were alone. There is a fact about air travel that important scientific researchers have spent millions of taxpayers' money to prove: a person traveling with a baby is about as welcome on an airplane as a gorilla. Oh, sure, everyone acts all nice, but just let a baby throw one little sippie cup and hit someone in the head, and suddenly your whole gate is afraid of you.

We coped, though, mainly by running up and down the "concourse" (translation: hallway) and yelling "shoe, shoe, shoe!" (new word).

Next, it was time to board the plane itself, which had pulled up outside and was getting its windshield washed. We had no trouble getting a seat alone—I marveled at that, but as I pulled crackers out of my hair and wiped juice from my clothes, I had to admit that sometimes things just work out.

The next step in the airplane experience is where the crew gets on the microphone and tells you all about the safety issues of your flight.

For example, in the unlikely event of a water landing, you are supposed to grab your seat (which is a float), unhook it somehow, turn it over, and float in the water with it until you are rescued by people looking for a lot of airplane seats floating in the water.

Now, at home I can't even fold a map, so I was not sharing the airline's vision of me working all this out. I studied the safety card tucked in the seatback in front of me—apparently if I had to be involved in any emergency scenarios I was to wear a concerned, but generally pleasant, expression on my face.

Soon, we were off! Unfortunately, once we were underway, the baby starting screaming "NO, NO!" over and over again. People on the plane were balling up their napkins and putting them in their ears. Some were putting peanuts in their ears instead of eating them.

When the beverage cart rattled by, the people near me were getting tiny little bottles and drinking them straight down.

"Soda's free!" I reminded the man across from me, but he couldn't hear me—he had peanuts in his ears.

So, we made it, in one piece.

The baby has been on an airplane.

And he has met someone who refers to him as "Precious," and he calls her "MaMaw," so that's all we need to say about that.

Q3

BELOVED CAPE COD

M Y FAMILY AND I have just gotten back from a week's vacation at Cape Cod. If I had to sub-title our week off together as a family, I would have to call it, *The Trip That Taught Me That I Live In A Sheltered Little Bubble.* Apparently, there is still a thing or two to be learned out there in the world.

It is a fact that as soon as the Reilly family—Papa Reilly, Mama Reilly, and kids, ages 14, 11, and 17 months—gets into a vehicle to go and enjoy some R and R together, it will start raining.

Not refreshing, contemplative drizzles—biblical rains. The kind of rain the news runs footage of where cars are submerged in canyons of water and traffic lights swing crazily in 100 mph winds. The kind of rain where I start out the trip with one kind of hairstyle—nice, fashionably flat—and at the beach emerge from my car with a humidity-induced Ronald McDonald Afro.

We were meeting some friends who were also staying at the Cape for a week, so we stopped by their beach cottage and over monsoon-like winds and rain yelled out plans to meet that night at their house for dinner .

"This is gonna be a great week!" my husband shouted to them, shielding his face from the stinging rain with a newspaper.

"The best ever, man!" our friend Scott yelled back, boarding up windows with plywood. Hey, we were on vacation, that's what counts.

Our family went to our friends' house for a celebratory "first-night-at-the-beach" dinner. All our kids got re-acquainted, I chatted with Scott's parents who were visiting overnight, and we all rejoiced in a temporary reprieve from the rain.

As my friend Pam brought dinner to the table, I felt a little flicker of alarm. She was setting a bowl of crustaceans on the table—lobsters, to be exact. Now, strange as it seems, I have only eaten "lazy man's" lobster—that is to say, I never see a shell; the lobster is already done for you by an unseen chef.

For years I thought lobsters morphed along the bottom of the ocean floor with cream sauce and paprika on their backs. That's the way I like it—I enjoy electricity, but I don't need to see how it runs through my walls.

There are two ways to go when you don't know what you're doing—admit it, saying loudly and jocularly, "Well, hey, I don't know what the heck I'm doing! I'm a fish out of water in this here situation!" Or, you can wing it and see how it goes. I decided to do that.

As a boiled lobster was plopped on my plate (crazy little eyeballs looking right at me), I continued my conversation with Scott's dad about the National Debt, while secretly watching everyone around me. They confidently ripped off heads and sliced through gullets with special tools.

There are tools for this? I thought, while saying, "Ed, debt is bad. No debt is good."

I had to start eating this thing, so I just kind of bent one of the lobster's arms back and started nibbling on his claw, hoping food would somehow pop out.

The conversation around the table died out—my own husband looked at me as if he were trying to remember who I was. Ed stared at me with a mixture of fascination and pity—the same look my sister and I used to have when my dad poured salt on slugs on the sidewalk. (Now, there's a skill you can actually use.)

Ed leaned forward and said, "Deirdre, what are you doing?"

A full lobster dangling from my mouth, I smiled and shrugged. "This is how we do it in my native land," I mumbled. (I'm from Maryland.) So, Ed nicely taught me how to "crack" a lobster.

Days of rain went by. Pam and I had wildly miscommunicated in the food department, so we had enough lasagna collectively to feed Cape Cod for a week. We wandered around our rental cottage memorizing the knick-knacks and eating lasagna. Then another chance to learn presented itself: we decided to go canoeing.

All of us (four grown-ups, four kids and a baby teething on a block of cold lasagna) showed up at the canoe-rental place and rented two canoes.

"Have you ever canoed before?" the lady at the dock asked us as we fitted ourselves for life preservers that would fit over lasagna-bloated stomachs.

"Oh, yes, we're what you might call canoe fanatics," my husband answered. We all turned to look at him—our teen-ager is the only one who canoes. My husband and I are not exactly extreme-sports types; the last outdoor activity we tried to do together was wrestling our old-fashioned TV antenna from our roof.

"Great," the lady answered, and we all hopped in. Canoeing is not as easy as you might think; hence the following sentences were heard from the Reilly canoe:

- "Hold on, this oar is going haywire!"
- "Why are we going in circles when everyone else is going straight? We keep seeing the dock over and over again!"

It's true; we were canoeing in circles. I was at the helm briefly, and birds started cawing annoyingly as I was trying to straighten us out, and you could almost hear them say to each other:

Red Alert. Suburban woman in red canoe approaching—wearing a Cape Cod sweatshirt, dan-

gling question-mark earrings, and wedgie sandals.
Danger—pass it on.

All too soon our vacation was at an end, and I reflected on what I had learned—as I packed our clothes, tucking wedges of lasagna among the clothes as another might tuck in a scented sachet. (Nothing says "romance" like a nightgown with clumps of lasagna on it.)

I had learned to canoe, and I had learned to crack a lobster. Rain or shine, it doesn't get any better than that.

℮

END OF SUMMER

I WISH I would have remembered, or I wish someone had reminded me, that when you have school-age children summertime is about eight months long.

"How's it going?" I'll say to a fellow parent, and he or she will look at me with glazed eyes and mumble, "School needs to start up again," before shuffling off down the street.

Two-thirds of the summer is now over, and my two older sons are keeping the same hours as vampires— very, very tired vampires. (You know how tiring it is getting all that sleep.)

At some time during the late morning they tumble down the stairs and into their seats where they sit and sigh a lot while I chant the mantra, "Next year we're doing camp all summer," while I get their breakfast.

The sleep-induced creases don't iron out of their faces until suppertime, and so help me, I'm jealous.

I'm up with our new baby at the crack of dawn, keeping farmer's hours. I can now assemble a wardrobe, make a gourmet meal, and dial overseas phone numbers in total darkness, but it's sleep I'm after.

"Oh—did I wake you—were you trying to rest?" I'll ask them as I perch on the edge of their beds playing a rousing rendition of "Home on the Range" on the accordion.

Conversely, these two boys are raring to go at night, when I'm keeping my eyes open with toothpicks. Boys who have fought for the last twelve hours straight and haven't been able to stand the sight of each other are suddenly as chummy as dentists at a convention when trying to obtain an extra half-hour of consciousness.

It is the great irony of my life that, while I am upstairs having cartoon-character hallucinations because I'm so tired, these boys, the fruit of our loins, are begging to stay awake so that they can play with the one person they've been trying to avoid like the plague all day.

My boys are also pretty bored at this point—they've been vacation-ed, museum-ed, aquarium-ed to death, according to them. When kids would lie motionless on the sofa and watch ninety-five hours of *Nickelodeon* on TV rather than go downtown and watch a diver in the aquarium tank swim amongst stingrays and whatnot, it's time to go back to school.

My oldest son has spent the bulk of the last few weeks trying to talk me into letting him see a horror movie called *The Blair Witch Project*, and he is as persistent as a tobacco lobbyist on Capitol Hill.

This piece of cinematic greatness, in defiance of all the big-money movies being made today, was made on a very small budget and features two hours of the view from a hand-held camera. I told my boys if they want scary I can run from bathroom to bathroom with our camera filming the toilets I haven't been able to clean since school let out in June. They passed on that.

I really shouldn't blame just the boys for having the end-of-summer malaise; the other night while watching TV we stumbled on a science fiction movie about a sad and blighted planet where all vegetation was dead and the ground was parched and intractable and my kids said, "Look, a movie about our yard!"

Okay, so we've kind of lost the will to garden, what with the drought and all—not that my yard doesn't look this way when there's not a drought. But we're still paying a yard service goo-gobs of money to come out and pour harmful chemicals over the ground— "Maybe Next Year" is this particular company's motto.

Mentally, by the end of August I'm ready for fall, while my husband loves summer and hates to see it go. If we happen to be invited to a party at the beginning of September he can be seen sporting flip-flops, a Hawaiian shirt and suntan lotion, while I'll be at his side wearing a turtleneck, hiking boots and carrying a pumpkin under my arm. We don't get invited to a lot of parties in September.

And so, we'll start to ready ourselves for the coming school year. I'll spend any amount necessary on school supplies, I'll send some flowers to the school principal, and I'll walk the route our kids will use to get to school, just to make sure there's nothing in their path that could impede their progress.

And I'll be a little sad, too, because the summer will be gone and next summer the boys will be just a little closer to all grown up.

That's okay, though. When they're in school it gives me more time to work on the yard. Or clean toilets— nah, I'll work on the yard.

CR

9 ∝∝

AND BABY MAKES FIVE

"... now that he can walk ...
he can also walk away."

∝

NEW BABY

FLASH BACK: SEVERAL months ago I was in the dry cleaner's dropping off some laundry and humming to myself, oddly serene. I was happy. My kids, one a preteen and one close to ten years old, had finally reached the age where they were somewhat self-sufficient, as well as being in school full days, leaving me plenty of time for myself. *Yep*, I thought, *I have really arrived. I've earned my stripes. Now is the time for "me."*

As I stood there congratulating myself, a young woman walked in holding a baby in her arms and coaxing a toddler through the door. Her hair was disheveled, her clothes seemed to be on sideways, and her glasses were hanging from one ear. Her baby was contentedly chewing on her shoulder, banging her on the head with a rattle shaped like a telephone, while her toddler screamed out the plot lines of a Barney episode.

She smiled at me and dropped her laundry on the counter. I smiled back, running my manicured fingernails through my freshly beauty-parlored hair. *I've come a long way, baby,* was what I was thinking. *It's time to get to know myself, to broaden my horizons, to "think outside the box." Me, me, me! A celebration of me!*

Flash forward: Two months later, I sat in the bathroom staring at the test wand, a huge plus sign staring back at me from the "indicator window."

I shook the wand, which was obviously broken. Still positive.

I threw it against the wall, then crawled under the sink to pick it up. Still positive.

I giggled maniacally. My cute little life evaporated in a fine pink-and-blue mist. I was going to have a baby. I therefore probably wouldn't be getting to know myself or be thinking outside the box anytime soon.

My husband took the news really well—after staring at me in stunned silence he went into optimistic mode, saying, "This is going to be all right" so many times I checked to see if he was, in fact, conscious. He sounded good, but I did find his wallet, keys, and beeper stacked neatly in the refrigerator the next day.

The first thing I did was cut my hair—probably an irrational hormonal response, although I am the only one who is allowed to say this. Each time I have been pregnant I have cut my hair several times. By the time I get to the delivery room I will look disturbingly like Yul Brenner yelling for drugs.

I went to my first doctor's appointment. I got up on the scale and the nurse yelled out my weight to another nurse while handing me a paper cup.

A month ago I had been surveying my lofty future, and now I was going to the bathroom in a Dixie cup and would be at least once a month for some time to come.

The doctor gave me an examination and pronounced me "advanced maternal," which is doctor code for "old lady having a baby." Gallons of blood were drawn at the lab (I reminded the technician that I might need some, too), and I went home.

We had to tell our boys. We assembled them in the family room, and I noticed how old they were, and how big. In fact, they seemed to take up every inch of available breathing space with their gigantic arms and legs, which seemed to trail off the couch and into the hall. A baby? What was going on here?

My husband told our happy news, and the boys looked at me as if I had just turned handsprings through the room. The look they gave each other said, "She's clearly unstable and cannot be trusted."

I pointed guiltily at their father—after all, he helped. We were then grounded and sent to our room while they discussed an appropriate punishment. The older son was thinking about what his parents had to do to become pregnant, while the younger one wondered aloud about the status of his private bedroom.

The food cravings and sickness began. I couldn't get enough eggs—my husband slumped up the sidewalk one evening after work only to be greeted by his crazed wife who grabbed his lapels and hissed, "If I don't get some egg salad soon, heads are gonna roll." A woman who had formerly been interested in art, literature, and music was now on a never-ending search for egg products.

The "morning" sickness lasted all day. My nights I spent on the bathroom floor, my head resting on the toilet seat, my face smiling every time one of the boys walked by, as if it was perfectly normal to be hanging over the toilet napping.

One such night my husband wandered in and began telling me about a sore knuckle on his hand that had been troubling him. A knuckle.

"Unless your knuckle is giving you the gift of a son or daughter in nine months I don't want to hear about it," I mumbled, closing the door on him.

And so it begins. We start to gear up for the baby toys, the diapers, the crib, and the late nights.

And, more importantly, the laughs, the fun and the joy.

And hopefully lots of eggs.

∞

TECHNOBABY

PROGRESS IS FOREVER rolling along, and right now it is rolling all over me, squashing me at every turn. Now pregnant with my third baby, and my second child being almost ten years old, almost every day I can see how I have unwittingly lagged far behind the rest of the human race when it comes to babies.

I decided to purchase some maternity clothes when I started getting some curious looks from friends and acquaintances, all directed at my waistline. I could see the questions flicker all over the polite person's face: *Is she in decline? Is she letting herself go? She must be; she's way too old to be pregnant!* And being sick of wearing unbuttoned pants, I decided to go shopping.

Things have certainly changed in the last ten years in the maternity wear department. Thirteen years ago, when I was pregnant with my first child, maternity clothes were just plain goofy.

At the time in my life when I was being called upon to be my most responsible and mature, I was dressed like Deirdre the Clown, with huge ruffles, collars, and bows everywhere on my person.

Now maternity clothes are stylish and demure—they're just gigantic versions of regular clothes. I walked into the store hesitantly, still not quite believing I was there.

"May I help you?" the genial woman at the counter asked, busy folding underwear the size of pillowcases into neat stacks.

"Umm . . . I'm just browsing," I said quickly.

Browsing? Maternity stores are like bait and tackle shops in one way: just being there implies intent to purchase, and not a lot of browsing is done at either.

Under her expert tutelage I bought a few new items including maternity bras that have the brand name "Leading Lady." Yep, that's exactly what I feel like as I stagger to the bathroom 14 times a night—a real leading lady. A couple of the tops I bought are the brand name "A Pea In The Pod"—no beating around the bush there.

Pregnancy has also been changed by medical technology. I was immediately apprised of a few tests that were available to us: maternal-serum alpha-fetoprotein screening, amniocentesis, and chorionic villis sampling (or CVS). I explained to the doctor that the only CVS I will be showing up for is the one that sells batteries and Snickers bars.

The amniocentesis is routinely offered to us old pregnant ladies, and it seemed that I could not have a conversation without being asked, "Are you having an amnio?" The first time someone asked me this I mistook "amnio" for "enema," and the rest of the conversation was quite intriguing.

As part of my prenatal care we were given a session of prenatal counseling at a state-of-the-art diagnostic center. My husband and I met in a room with a genetic counselor, who may have been a little frustrated at my lack of familial knowledge.

When asked what my ethnic heritage is I leaned back and mused, ". . . I think I have a little Dutch, or Danish, and I'm sure there's some farm stock because I have always felt a closeness to the land."

My husband, all puffed up because he got his answer right (how hard is it to remember "Irish"?), leaned forward in his chair and asked, "Could you, like, add traits to the baby? Could you make sure the baby is not chronically late? Also, throw in whatever it takes to keep the baby away from Halloween candy." He glanced at me sideways. The visit went well, and we left not knowing a thing more than when we came.

I also bought the newest pregnancy and childbirth guide. I now refer to this book as "Twenty Ways This Could Kill Me." There is a whole chapter about possible tragedies that can befall mother and baby entitled "When Something Goes Wrong."

What happened to good old Dr. Spock, who advised wearing supportive clothing and taking plenty of naps? Now *there* was a helpful book.

I started taking stock of my baby supplies for use after the baby comes. I currently have two dented rattles and a Gumby and Pokey sippie cup that I use as a back-up sugar bowl. I also have a crib at my sister-in-law's house in Connecticut and a car seat that would not pass the most measly of current requirements (there are also fossilized Cheerios all over it that would mystify any newborn).

My lack of baby things brought me to the brink of

despair—although this is easy to do these days what with my hourly mood swings.

One night I whined to my husband, "I have the feeling that you're feeling that my feelings aren't necessarily valid . . ."

How could the poor guy respond to that? First he had to decipher it. He responded to the lack of baby equipment with customary flair: "Pretend you're getting ready for my Christmas work party, honey. Start borrowing!" I have now lined up enough things for ten babies.

I did buy a baby monitor that my two boys are using as walkie-talkies when they play Army, so slowly the house will start to fill up with the evidence of our newest arrival.

Technology need not make me nervous—after all, women have babies in fields all the time, don't they? Okay, so maybe not in the fields of Reading, Massachusetts, but you know what I mean.

&

BABY JOINS THE FAMILY

A FEW WEEKS ago my family and I experienced a blessed event—the birth of our third child, James Paul Reilly.

Our first two children are older boys, one a teen-ager and one almost ten years old, so we are definitely diving back into the deep after a long time on the shore.

My labor was long and intense, punctuated by my husband asking, "Did that hurt?" at the end of each long and painful contraction. (Never ask a woman in labor or a dental patient having their gums scraped a question like that.)

Our baby finally arrived—a beautiful, healthy boy who stared at us bemusedly after his grand entrance. My husband, cradling him in his arms, confided to him, "You're already way ahead of the other babies, you know. You already have a dog, and you have two really big brothers. You're probably going to think they're uncles, because they're tall. I'll explain the concept of 'tall' to you later. Let's just say that the playground should never be a problem for you."

Our tiny pink bundle waved one fragile arm as if he understood.

I was now surrounded by males—males everywhere. My husband, father, and two older sons looked at the floor and screamed interesting weather facts to each other while a very enthusiastic nurse explained some finer points of breast feeding to me.

"Stop that laughing or leave, never to return . . . I love you all dearly," I laughed and cried, apparently in the grips of some hormonal postpartum mood swings.

"She's just got a little post-mortem," my teenage son explained to my nine-year-old, who nodded gravely.

"She's just got a little postmodernism," he in turn whispered knowingly to my husband, patting my hand.

By the time the message got to me it turned out that I had a very normal, short-term case of "post office." The baby and I looked at each other and sighed.

Leaving the hospital was a spectacle. I had only been there two days and was bringing home a person not even two-feet long, and my family looked like a band of nomadic gypsies carrying everything they owned on their backs (very nice, cuddly nomadic gypsies who favored bunny and duckie motifs).

Diaper bags slung over shoulders, arms filled with

blankets, baby carriers and pounds of educational material, we staggered out of the hospital and to the car. All this for a person who had spent the last nine months totally naked.

One thing about babies—they change everything. We had to learn to be quiet—so we spent the majority of the first full day at home from the hospital speaking in sign language to each other while staring anxiously at the baby.

It's pretty hard to sign, "Honey, will you get me some cookies; not the SnackWell's cookies but the cookies that your mom made that you liked when she brought them to that party that time," but we did our best.

Babies also make grown-ups act goofy. It's electrifying to see your tax consultant lean over a bassinet in a business suit and say, "Well! Wicky Wicky Woo Woo to you, too, mister!" in between telling you about some serious tax shelters.

I really miss sleep. The baby is already bored with our house, as we have walked around it 18,000 times in our quest to get comfortable and sleepy. Yesterday he actually suggested a bolder look for the front hallway.

Early one morning as he changed the baby, my husband idly mentioned going over the household bills after I ran in, exhausted and haggard, and said, "Pay the cable! I don't care if we don't have water, heat, or town services, but pay that cable bill! The baby and I are watching *Biography* on A&E; it's *Big Losers* week."

My husband looked at me pointedly as if to say, *Are you on the show this week?* At the time I was wearing a bathrobe, huge sweatpants, and loafers. When you're up all night you tend to amass layers of clothing, and matching is not an issue.

And as we adjust, we change, all of us together. And we have another boy. Another boy to lie in the grass and study bugs with. Another boy to toss a baseball to on a twilight summer evening and hear his delighted, "Dad, I caught it!" the first time he does.

Another boy to whom, no matter if he's four, or 14, or 40, we'll whisper, "Be careful," as he walks away.

Another boy that all too soon, I now know, we'll have to start to let go of. But that is another day.

So, newest boy, put your tiny hand in all our larger ones and together . . . we begin.

CR

NEW BABY TOYS

WE HAVE A new baby in our family, which means that we have been learning a lot lately about the newest trends in baby care.

Thirteen years ago, when we had our first baby, things seemed to be a lot simpler—those were the good old days when you put a baby on the couch to sleep if you were out visiting—you didn't have to lug along a "Pack 'N' Play" for the baby to hang out in (and incidentally it's nicer than the interior of my house).

One of the things I received for the baby at my baby shower was a "baby gym"—which officially makes the baby the only member of the family who goes to a gym. It's a mat that the baby lies on, and overhead little objects dangle down to attract his attention.

While I have to tape canned vegetables to my ankles to get a workout around here, the baby is attending a state-of-the-art facility right on my family room floor. All this for a person who is totally entertained by a lamp cord.

Another thing that is new is car seats and the placement of them in the car. When my other kids were little, babies rode up in the front seat, facing backward. Due to advances in baby safety, babies now ride in the backseat facing backward—and hence my baby could not be more isolated from me if he were growing up in the laundry room.

I spend all our time out in the car pulling up to drive-thru windows and asking the drive-thru person things like, "Say, will you look in the backseat and check on the baby? Is he doing all right—could you possibly give him this pacifier? Sure, I'll order a Coke."

There's a little mirror you can buy that you can angle in front of the baby, attaching it to the backseat, so that you, the driver, can look in your rearview mirror and see that mirror reflecting your baby's face, thereby ascertaining how your baby is doing without ever actually seeing your baby. Huh? I still can't adjust my regular car mirrors by myself, and they want me to do this? The picture on the box that this mirror came in has arrows pointing everywhere to explain how this works and looks like a Pink Floyd light show. I just pull over every three miles to see the baby in person.

We have a car seat that also turns into a stroller and a baby-carrier—the baby is so baffled he keeps looking at me to see what else *I* can turn into. When we bought it the very polite salesman asked us what we wanted from a car seat. My husband and I looked at each other blankly.

"We'd, uh, I don't know, like it to hold the baby while we're in the car," we said hesitantly, and the salesman smiled knowingly.

"You need the BabyMaster 900," he explained, dragging a car seat from a display case and right before our astonished eyes turning it into a stroller.

"Well, Jeepers," we muttered, immediately sold on it.

So, I'm building muscles the size of volleyballs yanking the car seat out of the car every time we go for a walk or the baby needs to sit in a seat inside. But we're on the cutting edge.

When assembling my baby items before the baby's birth, I went to buy a thermometer, and was astonished at the choices I had. Besides the good old rectal thermometer, you can now buy a digital oral thermometer, a thermometer you stick in your ear, even a digital oral pacifier thermometer for babies.

I ended up going home with the old fashioned thermometer—it doesn't really matter, because we'll lose it in the house and end up at an all-night drugstore in our pajamas just when we really need it.

We purchased a battery-operated baby swing, and it has become the most important possession we own. I would gladly give up my car, house and television—just let me keep the swing that keeps the baby happy. It is not unusual for one of our older kids to wander into the family room and, gesturing towards the baby happily asleep in the swing, ask, "So, what speed is he on?"

We are accumulating more cute, modern baby stuff by the minute for the only member of the house that has no interest at all in such things.

But the old stand-bys still apply; he, like all babies before him, still loves to be sung to, carried around on a comfortable shoulder, and rocked to sleep.

I don't know though; I did see a tiny baby chaise lounge that looked pretty cute; we must have room for it somewhere.

CR

OLD AND PARENTING

HAVING A NEW baby is a lot different than it used to be, back when I was young and could stay up past 9:30 at night. When I had my first two kids—disco was in then—I zipped through my busy days and was still raring to go at night. With this, our third baby, things are different; I'm old.

For one thing, my mind is shot. I burst into tears recently because I couldn't remember how to work the *TV Guide.*

"You're just tired," my husband consoled me, helping to fold the thirtieth load of laundry for the day. (Unfortunately, I had added a bit too much detergent to this particular load—I must have forgotten I had added it, so I added it over and over again—and the clothes were so stiff it was like trying to fold hubcaps. Let's just say that my kids couldn't find their Frisbee so they tossed a washcloth back and forth to each other.)

I am tired. I was reading a magazine that featured stories on both lotto winners and a town that suffered a bad flu epidemic, and I was jealous of the town. Hey, they got to rest.

Physically I'd say I've changed in the last ten years. After I line up the baby bottles in the refrigerator at night in preparation for the next day, I line up my medications for the next day.

I bent over to pick the baby up one morning and stayed in that position for the rest of the day—bad back kicking in. It looked as if the baby were being raised by an orangutan.

"Babies keep you young," a neighbor called out to

me as I shuffled by with the stroller, too tired to push it over level ground.

The kids jumped in to help, rigging up a sled-like contraption that utilized levers, pulleys, and the family dog, but I discouraged that, waving them off and wiping drool off my shirt—unfortunately it was my drool and not the baby's.

"Now, who planted shrubs in the middle of the street?" I asked my husband irritably one evening, standing on the porch and burping the baby.

"Those are our kids, honey," my husband answered, quickly taking the baby. "I'll get your glasses."

Fortunately, our baby has started sleeping through the night, so I was able to take off the pacifier necklace I was getting so many comments on.

In truth I think the baby kind of gave up, it was taking me so long to get to his cradle in the middle of the night—I had to straighten out my sciatic leg, unkink my back, grab my glasses, rub my neck, stomp one foot (charley-horse cramps), and stagger towards the nightlight.

My husband, who prior to the baby's birth would wake up if I dropped a cotton ball in the basement, slept through all this each night.

The extra weight I gained during this last pregnancy is not exactly falling off, either. I was in the sporting goods store with my older two boys and a well-meaning clerk, no doubt impressed by my thighs and my stooped posture, brought me a pair of speed skates to try on. If I throw one hand behind my back I could be mistaken for Dan Jansen.

I guess I'll have to get out of a little private rhythm I've started for myself: change the baby/have an Oreo. Make a bottle for baby/have an Oreo. Do baby's laundry/have an Oreo.

Then there is the timeless question often asked of us older parents: "Did you realize that by the time the baby is 25 years old, you'll be over 60?"

A vision is immediately brought to mind of a forlorn young man gingerly throwing a baseball to two people who fall over their canes and walkers trying to catch it.

What exactly does the baby need us to be young for?

Young men over 20 actually spend very little time down at the neighborhood park throwing a baseball—from what I hear they're too busy making their parents' hair fall out in clumps by not looking into a 401(k) or by choosing an unsuitable life partner.

So, we consider ourselves ahead of the game. Our hair will probably already be disappearing (along with our teeth) when this baby starts to worry us, so we might as well not fret over it.

I actually have a more pressing issue: has anyone seen my glasses, my medication, or both?

∽

BABY'S BIRTHDAY

WE HAVE A baby who will be a year old this week, and as I look around, I realize how much life has changed in that one year. Particularly my life, being the mom.

I talk a lot of baby talk now—the exterminator called me to tell me about a complicated chemical process we are going to use to get rid of our carpenter ants, and I answered in a high, squeaky voice, "Now aren't you a smart boy! How clever! Good for you! We'll

get rid of mean old Mister Ant and then have a snack!"
He seemed a little confused.

I'm the one that's confused—my older boys had a
week off from school recently, and I started to talk like
they do. My husband came home from work one night
that week and told me the porch light had burned out,
to which I replied, without taking my eyes off the video
game I was playing, "Bummer."

He asked me how a neighbor of ours was doing,
and I replied, "Oh, what's-her-face? She's, like, good."

A friend came over to go to the mall with me, and
my husband listened to me tell her about a new store
that is "totally wicked awesome"; then I tightened my
stomach and said to her, "Go on. See how hard you
can hit me." I needed some time away from the boys.

Your life slows down in some ways when you have
a baby around—I can't seem to get myself off our
hallway stairs.

The baby is learning to go up stairs, so that's
where he spends the majority of his time and effort.
And I'm right behind him.

And he likes to spend a little time on each stair,
just getting comfortable. So I spend a little time on
each stair.

The dog spends her time one stair below us, because
she's afraid that I love the baby more that I love her.

That's where you can find us between the hours of
7 a.m. and 7 p.m. It's no wonder my husband comes
home to crying jags and detailed descriptions of how
dirty our hall walls are.

You also spend a lot of time trying to get the baby
to talk on the phone to relatives in that first year. Your
objective when on the phone is to make as many
funny, frantic faces at the baby as your facial muscles
will let you without pain in order to make him utter

anything—a grunt, a sound, anything. The baby's objective is to pull the phone away from his face and look at all the numbers all lit up.

The person on the other end never knows when the baby is actually "on" the phone, so you can hear a lot of interesting things when you put the phone back to your own ear.

A sure way to make a baby say a word for the first time is to hang up with a relative who was on a ship-to-shore phone from Alaska and who spent hundreds of dollars trying to talk to the baby. The baby will stare at you with his mouth hanging open for the entire phone call, but hang up the phone and he will say, "Cow, ducky, pig," and toddle away.

Another interesting thing happens to parents of a baby—they lose all sense of modesty. Our teen-ager has witnessed this first-hand, and he's not too impressed with what he's seen. I came in one evening, and my husband flew down the stairs.

"The baby had a weird poop," he said, concerned. Our teen-ager just sat there, listening.

"Did you save it?" I asked, quickly shedding my coat.

"Yes, it's upstairs," my husband said, sounding like a researcher talking to a colleague. "See what you think."

After parental analysis of the poop, it was determined that corn was the culprit, and it was our teen-ager's analysis that we have lost our minds.

You spend a lot of time looking silly when you're a parent. I was at a stoplight recently belting out the words to a children's music tape, singing to the baby in the backseat, when I realized that the man pulled up next to me was watching me sing, but couldn't see that I had a baby in the car. So from his perspective I was animatedly singing "It's My Bathtime" to myself.

It's been a wonderful year. A magical year of baby teeth, soft blankets, nightlights, and mobiles.

A year of midnight snuggles, a soft, warm head on my shoulder, and first steps. Only with this baby's first steps, as the family cheered, his mother, standing to the side, shed a few tears.

She knows that now that he can walk . . . he can also walk away.

Happy Birthday, honey.

რ

TIME OFF

RECENTLY, MY HUSBAND and I took our annual trip alone together—by annual, I mean about once every three or four years. I have a nursery rhyme to thank for this year's trip, strangely enough.

We have three kids, ages 14, 11, and 20 months old, and let's just say that at this point in everyone's development I am physically, emotionally, and mentally exhausted.

The older two are mentally exhausting—as I was innocently minding my own business, trying to read a little of my *People* magazine, my older son said conversationally, "Do you and Dad realize that as consumers you have become duped by the corporate machinery into thinking that your needs outweigh your wants?"

I turned the page and said, "Thank you, honey—I'll let Dad know."

My 11-year-old is a blur of activities, one blending

right into the next—he and I both have upholstery patterns on our backs from so much time in the car. My left hand is significantly stronger that my right due to being handed so much fast food through my car window. The whole neighborhood calls me when they need a jar opened. It's scary.

The baby, on the other hand, is pretty tiring in his own right. He is at the "mommie" stage, when he likes for me to be by his side day and night.

One day, as I had escaped into the bathroom for a minute with my *People* magazine, I saw something out of the corner of my eye and realized that the baby had thoughtfully slipped his favorite nursery rhyme book under the bathroom door for me, and I knew he was waiting patiently on the other side.

This nursery rhyme book is actually a musical book, so you can sing along with a rhyme just by pushing a button. Unfortunately, the battery is wearing out, so you get a bleary, depressing little tune as you try to sing along.

One song, in particular, caught the baby's attention:

> Oats, peas, beans and barley grow,
> Oats, peas, beans and barley grow,
> Do you, or I, or anyone know
> How oats, peas, beans and barley grow?

The whole family was stuck on this nursery rhyme, and it proved to be my undoing.

One day, as I swiped at the counter with a ratty old sponge—the same counter I had wiped down thirty times already—my husband called.

"Do you, or I, or anyone really know," I said, in a voice that Eeyore from *Winnie the Pooh* would be proud of, "how oats, peas, beans or barley grows?"

My husband said, "I'm calling my mother—you and

I are going to go away for the weekend."

So, that's how we got the weekend away. Now, you would think that everything would have been hunky-dory with us, now that we were leaving town. Oh no—marriage is much too complicated for that. I think in the wedding vows somewhere it actually says, "Do you promise to love, honor, and cherish one another? Do you promise to forsake all others? Do you promise to argue for a good hour or so on your way up to Loon Mountain on your weekend away together?"

That's how it goes when you have two exhausted people who finally get in a car alone to decompress for two hours.

On our last trip up North alone, we stayed at a quaint Bed and Breakfast and did some hiking, prancing along trails in our leather coats, sneakers, and earmuffs; but this time, the plan was different. This time, we were going to take it easy.

We stayed at a regular hotel, which was really kind of soothing in its anonymity. My husband was all grins as he flopped on the bed, immediately thrilled with a remote control that you didn't have to bang against your leg to get to work.

I checked out the bathroom. What is really strange about modern hotel bathrooms is that there is a telephone right on the wall near the toilet. There are just not that many people I need to talk to that badly. Do business travelers really need this?

I can just picture a business man sitting on the toilet with work papers spread out along the sink saying, "Yeah, Bob, hi—Dan from Ace Printing here. Listen, I'm calling you back with that pricing. Where am I? Actually I'm sitting on the toilet in a hotel room right off I-93. Hello? Hello?"

I was tempted to pick up the phone myself, but I

was halfway afraid that the blurry music from "Oats, peas, beans and barley" would come through the receiver, like in a horror movie.

There was also a hair dryer in the room which had two drastically varying speeds: "Infant Breathing on You" and "Caught in a Killer Wind Tunnel."

I came out to the main room, where my husband was eerily engrossed in the movie *Grease II* on cable. Still decompressing, I guessed.

So, we watched movies, ate a lot of food, window-shopped, and took a minute to enjoy the view. And realized that some day, we will have as much alone time as we want. I can read all the magazines I can get my hands on. No one will be bothering us with their comments, their activities, or their musical nursery rhyme books.

We got home as fast as we could.

CR

10 ങ്ങ

CAR LIFE

"The clicking is happening
because the tires are cold."

ങ

I USED TO WALK FIVE MILES
TO SCHOOL

MY CAR HAS been in the shop undergoing repairs for the past two weeks, and it has tested my family in ways I never would have dreamed—tested our creativity, our endurance, and our ability to be forced together for extended periods of time. In short, it's been murder on us all.

I suppose I had warnings that my vehicle—a large, older-model Jeep—might spend a fair amount of time suspended over a team of mechanics when we went to purchase it—we just ignored these warning signs. At the time I was pretty excited because, although we were in the used car market, this was to be my vehicle, and I had never before owned a car that had been manufactured before prohibition. I also had a choice between mini-van and Jeep, because somehow a family of four these days does not even think of "squeezing" into a regular car.

Now, as any thirty-something was glad to tell me, mini-van says, *Hello, my life is effectively over. I cart kids and groceries around all day and while I live a life full of purpose, it's boring,* while truck says, *What's up! Yeah, I've got the kids in the back, but I may also do some 4-wheeling or camping later on, if I want to, depending on my very sharp yuppie instincts.* I opted for the, although delusional, highly hopeful Jeep.

We found the Jeep we wanted in the classified ads and drove to a whole other state to look at this used vehicle. Although the seller was technically a used car salesman, this place was less "car lot" and more "big yard with a couple of cars parked in it." I tried to maintain a neutral buyer's attitude, and so was properly wary when looking at the vehicle, although I think my sharp investigative questions reflected how long it had been since I had bought a car.

"So," I asked haughtily, upon inspecting the interior of the truck, "where is the eight-track tape player?" I tapped my fingers on the dash impatiently.

"Well, vehicles now seem to come with either the cassette deck or CD player unit," the seller said, loosening his tie and mopping his brow. I turned to my husband—how would I listen to my Seals & Crofts tapes driving around in this thing?

"Well," I asked a few minutes later, "how do you roll up these windows? Where's the window crank?"

"It's been a while since we purchased a car," my husband coughed, scanning the horizon as if a new, intelligent wife was going to appear.

Then came the test drive—my husband and I decided we loved it, and my kids decided they could be seen in it. The only little problem was a persistent clicking sound somewhere in the front end. When we got back to the car lot, my husband questioned the seller about this.

"Oh, the clicking?" he said, waving our concerns away with a hand that was incidentally holding a purchase agreement. "The clicking is happening because the tires are cold."

Cold tires? We all looked at each other blankly, and the seller beamed at us all. The vehicle was ours.

The Jeep, or "family truckster," as it is affectionately known, has been a good around-town vehicle, although the clicking has sometimes reappeared. Even, to our astonishment, when the tires are not cold. And like any family who cannot afford costly repairs, we simply and pointedly ignore it. When it clicks, we turn up the radio or talk louder, silently willing it to go away.

Gradually other bad sounds have joined the clicking, and now the truck is in for repairs, leaving me and the kids temporarily without any transportation. Don't worry, I assured my pouting kids, this will be a new experience for us. We'll walk everywhere, like a hiking team, only we won't hike through woods, or build campfires, or have any hope of actual fun.

We've made it through the dragging weeks so far, doing old-fashioned things like hanging around the house playing board games, making cookies (about 400 or so), and talking.

My kids were amazed that vocal cords work for more than 30 seconds at a time when aimed at an adult. When I first brought out the Scrabble board they eyed me suspiciously. Then they fell all over me and gave me huge, pitying hugs, amazed that I was forced to live in The Age Before Video Games.

Enough is enough, though. We will welcome our old truck back with open arms; we'll even run her through the car wash. After all, we feel, what's a little clicking among family?

CR

OLD CAR

SINCE THE ECONOMY seems to be taking a little downward turn, our family has had to tighten the old belt a little bit and stretch what we have just a little further.

The other day I caught myself telling my kids to eat the heels of the bread because "that's where the vitamins are." Our two-year-old looks like a Victorian baby because all his pants are now up to his knees and resemble knickers. I just speak in a British accent and call him "Reginald, darling," when we're out at the mall or the supermarket.

The other day I proudly passed up a sale on some plush-plush bath towels—we'll keep on using our old towels, even if there are a few beach towels in the rotation. There's nothing like seeing a businessman, fresh from the morning's shower, talking shop on the phone ("Now, Mike, let's float the expansion idea and flatline Option B on those margins . . .") while wrapped in a *Josie and the Pussycats* beach towel. But the most disappointing news was that now is not the time to replace my old Jeep.

This Jeep is old. Things are falling off it. The rubber handle for the turn signal arm is in my silverware drawer, the volume knob for the radio is in my diaper bag, and a neighbor thoughtfully returned a long chrome strip that apparently ripped off when I backed out of the driveway and scraped our old bushes. (Sometimes when I can't sleep I mentally put all these things back where they belong on the vehicle and then sleep like a baby for 12 hours.)

In the back of the Jeep I have old Hefty bags of clothes that I keep meaning to take to the Salvation Army drop site, enough rusty tools to stop by an archaeological dig and actively participate, and two sleds that, from the way they are jammed in back there, give the appearance of one long surfboard.

I also have interesting things adorning the outside; I pulled up in the church parking lot last Sunday with, unbeknownst to me, a plastic sword balanced across the bumper, like a challenge. I have ice scrapers under the seats I can only locate in the summertime, and enough fossilized French fries wedged everywhere to build a town with.

There are a lot of things on the old Jeep that just don't work anymore. One radio speaker was blown ages ago, so that all you hear when riding along is static with a few desperate-sounding voices eking through, but we obediently turn the radio on every time we get in the car, anyway.

The wipers drag along the windshield in the rain actually pushing *more* water into my line of vision.

One of the hardest things to deal with, though, is the broken defroster. I can't see a thing through my windshield unless the car has been actively running for about two hours.

In the cold weather we inch along in the morning on our way to school like a military tank in *The Dirty Dozen*, the kids yelling coordinates to me while I desperately try to see out of the one little circle I have rubbed out with my hands.

"Careful, Mom, move to your left a little—we are now approaching the Millers' mailbox with about a two-foot gap in clearance. Clear sailing after that," my oldest son reports, adjusting his headset and consulting his radar screen.

My next son gathers old French fries to try to fashion them into some sort of scraper so that I can make it safely home. By the time I pull back into the driveway, my windshield is perfectly clear.

The worst thing about the Jeep, though, is the gas gauge. It broke about two years ago, and back then I took it in stride.

"Look, it's simple," I told my husband. "I'll just write down my mileage on a napkin or envelope in the glove box, and when I've gone 150 miles, I'll get gas!" (Another option would have been to fix the gas gauge.)

Well, my method worked, for a little while. But soon I forgot about the napkin, and plus—people *use* napkins.

One night a friend reached for The Napkin to wipe her mouth with while saying, ". . . and what I learned about life through that experience was . . ." and all I could think was, *There goes my mileage.*

So, I run out of gas a lot. My husband is always sympathetic—from the safety of his sporty little perfectly-working car he'll say over the car phone, "But what about the mileage napkin? Isn't that our method?"

Before I hang up on him I say, "Napkins! What are we, insane? Who uses napkins for their gas gauge? Napkins make good napkins—but they're no gas gauge!"

We'll have to hang on a bit longer. *Soon*, we promise ourselves.

"We'll have to take our time picking out a new car, though," I warn my husband as I put the radio knob back on, consult the mileage napkin, and brush the old French fries away as I pull out of the driveway. "I'm pretty choosy!"

CR

MILEAGE NAPKIN

THE LAST TIME you read the words contained in this space, you might remember that you read about my old truck and how many things are going wrong with it. It doesn't heat up when you need it to, it doesn't cool down when you need it to, buttons and knobs are falling off of it, it doesn't defrost in any reasonable period of time, and the list goes on and on.

Apparently, one of the many problems with my vehicle struck a chord with some readers, and that is the broken gas gauge and my need to use what we in my family refer to as the Mileage Napkin. Simply put, the Mileage Napkin is the napkin I keep in the glove box that I write my mileage on and the mileage at which I will need to get gas.

"Explain the Mileage Napkin, Deirdre, and be more specific" is what I've heard a lot the past couple of weeks. So here is my humble attempt to explain the Mileage Napkin.

First, it goes without saying, your gas gauge should be inoperable. Otherwise, this would all be pointless and silly.

Second, you need to get a bunch of napkins from someplace like Dunkin' Donuts. Just walk on in, order yourself a nice donut or something, and grab a sizeable wad of napkins while you're waiting. They don't mind;

frankly, they're so busy trying to sell something called a Dunkaccino that they've got their hands full.

If you aren't near a Dunkin' Donuts or you just keep forgetting, simply grab an envelope or, better yet, a piece of mail like a really important bill or your car registration renewal or something, to substitute for the napkin. My method is nothing if not adaptable.

The point is, the piece of mail should cause a sick feeling, caused by numbing depression every time you handle it, because it's a constant draining reminder of yet another thing you're not doing, or taking care of, or handling right.

Anyway, just slide that old napkin or envelope into the glove box directly on top of the gum wrappers, maps, smudged sunglasses, old unraveled cassette tapes, and rusty green pennies stuck to the laminate, and you are almost good to go.

You will just need one more thing, and you are on your way to self-sufficiency like you've never known before; you'll look at a stranger in the next lane glancing casually at his perfect little gas gauge with its pointy little needle and think to yourself, *'Yuppie!' Just one of the mindless high-tech masses yearning for they know not what. I think I'll go home and knit a quilt for the family!*

The one thing you'll still need is a writing utensil. Now don't get all fancy and invest a lot of money in this part; a simple broken pencil or an old-fashioned ballpoint pen will do just fine.

I personally use a ballpoint pen that has something wrong with it; you click the clicker at the top and nothing happens. So, I simply unscrew the pen at the middle and then screw it back up again. Apparently when air gets to the middle of the pen it's rejuvenating to the ink, or something.

Don't worry too much if you do go with a broken

ballpoint pen for your writing utensil; your mileage and just about anything you write on your Mileage Napkin will be carved into your thigh for the next half-hour or so if you lean on your leg to write.

You are ready to fly! To test your napkin, simply start driving until you run out of gas. I personally run out of gas where it is dark and scary and things that look like alien spaceships hover right over my car, but this part is really different for each person.

So, get towed to the gas station and confidently say, "Fill 'er up, good sir!"

Now, while the attendant is filling up the tank, locate your Mileage Napkin. Find your ballpoint open in the mess that is your glove box, and start trying to scratch numbers onto your napkin while squinting in the dark.

You have three options here:

1) Either write down what your mileage is currently, after you've filled the tank, or

2) Write down what your actual mileage will be when you next need gas, or

3) Write your name backwards in bubble letters followed by exclamation points, having forgotten all about your mission.

Then, simply stow the napkin in the glove box, and be on your way.

A few reminders: do not forget to circle the latest mileage count on your napkin, as it will fill up with non-sensical looking numbers pretty quickly, and do not use your Mileage Napkin to check your oil. Enough said. Now you go grab a Dunkaccino and have a great day!

CR

11 ങ്ക

SPECIAL DAYS

"And so, on the streets of the North End of Boston, as people milled about and delivery trucks came and went, good will fell over a small part of the big city, and there was the feeling of Christmas."

ങ

A Christmas Trilogy

ങ്ക

CHRISTMAS TREE

IT'S HOLIDAY TIME again—that time of year when my husband stands in the yard untangling yards of decorative lights while watching football through the family room windows. The time of year when we assemble toys with 10,000 screws, using a butter knife. This year it's the time of year to avoid anyone who might use the word "Furby."

In the spirit of the season our family was invited by some friends to go and cut down our Christmas tree at a nearby farm. Being pregnant and exhausted, I would have been happy to order our tree over the Internet, but this was a great reason to get out of the house and enforce some family time with our two boys.

So, we happily accepted and planned to join our friends in doing something we have never done— murder a tree. We have always bought ours at a tree lot where you can get not only a tree but also gas, snacks, and air for the car tires. The tree is already cut and waiting; we just have to load it into the car.

Now, there is one fundamental problem with this new experience—you should never give the Reillys a job that involves handing them a saw. We simply are not hardy people; we love cable TV, and I dust our ATM cards weekly to keep them in prime condition. To give us the opportunity to tramp around a forest like we have any idea what we're doing is to ask for trouble.

My husband happily donned his work gloves (they still have the plastic price tag on them) and pulled our big old Jeep out onto the street. The kids shuffled into the car, complaining. Why go see real nature when you can probably find some on TV?

My husband turned to all of us. "Should I bring the saw?" he asked.

"Yes, unless you want to bend the Christmas tree down," my preteen commented, tuning the car radio to his station. My husband returned from the garage holding the saw tentatively (if there is such a thing as holding a saw tentatively). After all, we have never cut down a tree before, at least not on purpose. I checked to make sure I had our health insurance card, and we were off.

We met our friends at a picturesque farm that featured rolling hills dotted with all kinds of trees. At the end of a gravel parking area was a little shack where two men were handing out saws to suburbanites just like us who couldn't wait to get their hands on them. Grown men in crisp lumberjack shirts with cell phones in the pockets gazed at the saws admiringly, then looked out at the acres of trees. *With God as my witness, I'm going to bag a tree with a 200-ornament capacity or else!* their determined looks said.

The kids scattered to play in the trees, and we set out to do our work. My husband turns out to be the pickiest tree-chooser in the history of the world.

"Good circumference, nice branch spread," he mumbled, circling each candidate. "Whoa, there, what's this? A bald spot. Let's move on." Trees actually wilted under his criticism as he passed by, their branches swooping to the ground in defeat.

Other families seemed to be having similar problems; wives dragged children out of trees while men trudged up and down aisles of trees looking around like madmen, afraid to miss the perfect tree. My husband somehow shrunk our house in his mind and was considering trees that came up to his knee in height.

"We don't want it to touch the ceiling; that means sawing either at the top or the bottom," he muttered to himself, while actually leaning over to look at the top of the prospective tree.

I, on the other hand, was thrilled to find the perfect tree until my husband pointed out that the tree I had my eye on wasn't even part of the farm but was on the edge of a real forest and was about 200 feet in height.

At one point I grabbed the saw and set out on my own, determined to cut down the first tree I saw, my one criterion being that it had to have branches.

There is surely no more daunting sight than an obviously pregnant woman wielding a saw. Wildlife were suddenly quiet, children started behaving, and suddenly quiet, children started behaving, and the ozone layer spontaneously repaired itself as I walked by.

I went up to the first tree in my path and called to my husband to come and see it. I groaned as he came into view shaking his head, not impressed with my choice.

"I'm going to go cut down a wreath," I sighed, leaving Paul Bunyan to his deliberations.

At the main farmhouse there was a gift store (a sure sign of a working farm), and I waited there, drinking free apple cider.

My family soon returned, dragging their prey proudly behind them, and no one was bleeding, so I was happy. We had a wonderful time with our friends, and the tree was, indeed, perfect.

Now, if the Reillys can cut down a tree in the woods without killing themselves, world peace shouldn't be that hard, should it?

ର୍ଷାର୍ଷ

CHRISTMAS ONLINE

THE CHRISTMAS HOLIDAYS are here. Time to tear apart the attic looking for Christmas lights, only to get them all wound around the porch and the shrubs and discover that one teeny, tiny bulb is missing, resulting in absolute darkness.

There is nothing quite as deflating as assembling the whole family on the lawn (the kids craning their necks trying to see the TV through the house windows) and uttering those famous words, "Ready? Here we go!" only to have nothing happen.

"Did you test the lights?" I ask my husband, who by this time is about as receptive to this question as he is to the question, "Do we really need ESPN in our cable package?"

I am one of those people who are easily worn out by the preparations for Christmas. I can be found at the mall on Christmas Eve, crazily scanning the storefronts, desperately mumbling things to myself like, "Aunt Edith liked that ashtray I made her in second grade—I think I'll buy her a kiln," or "I think Mom would look good in a tiara."

With the advent of cell phones, shopping gets even crazier: I called my dad from the mall using a cell phone, and—trying to muffle the sounds of the monstrous water fountain I was standing next to—said, "Hey, Dad, it's me. How's it goin'? Say, have you measured your neck lately? I was just wondering."

Invariably as I'm running from store to store like a rooster on caffeine I run into an "organized friend." This friend, who has been finished shopping for weeks, is waltzing down the lane, stopping to admire the poinsettias and rearranging her smart-looking Christmas scarf—the one with the reindeer jumping all over it.

"Hey," I say, running up to her. "Take one of these bags before my circulation is gone for good." I extend a bag with an arm that is claw-like and blue from carrying bags of toys, clothes, and electronics. "What are you here for?" I puff.

"Oh, well, let's see," she muses, taking a list decorated with hand-stenciled reindeer (the same reindeer on the scarf) and scanning it. "A white taper candle and a gold bow," she answers. You don't say.

I decided to avoid all that this year. I have a

computer, and I decided to shop "online." I was thrilled—except that you have to use the computer to do it.

I approach our home computer as a large game hunter approaches his prey (I actually wear the orange vest and the hat with the earflaps): very warily and respectfully, knowing it could do me permanent damage.

"Well, I'm ready! Here we go!" I say loudly to my family, who are milling around nearby. "Time to use technology to save money and time!"

Now, there's one thing that online shopping is: lonely. At the mall, even with the craziness and the crowds, you're with people. Even if you go alone, you're with people. At the computer, even though I had the Christmas music going and the glass of eggnog on the desk, I was still alone.

"Hey, want to sit with me while I'm on the computer?" I said to my ten-year-old, who was passing by.

"Are you shooting down enemy planes or tramping through alligator-infested swamps?" he asked, peering at the screen.

"Well, no, but I'm buying your Grandma some flannel underwear online," I answered.

"No thanks," was his quick reply.

"Hey, I'll buy you an extra present if you sit with me for five minutes," I said to my teen-ager, who was sitting in the other room.

"Only if I can enter a chat room and 'I.M.' all my friends," he yelled back. Not having a hope in this world of deciphering what he said, I gave up on him.

My husband walked in from the store after I had been at it for about an hour.

"Honey!" I yelled, jumping out of my chair. "How are you? We never talk anymore—how do you feel your work at your company is going—aesthetically, I mean. Are you reaching goals that make you feel good about you?"

He stepped back, his brow furrowed as if he didn't recognize me (it's true I was bloated from gallons of eggnog and about ten million little Christmas candies) and set his bags down.

"How was the grocery store?" I enquired, ready to chat.

"You wouldn't believe how crowded it was," he replied, ". . . hey, where are you going?"

"There're people there—people who talk?" I asked over my shoulder. "I'll be home soon!"

And so, we learn.

I've learned that even though it's crazy out at the malls and in the stores, at least people are gathered together.

I've learned that Christmas means people, not presents.

And I've learned that you can wipe out all of your husband's computer files if you don't exit off of the computer the right way.

So, Merry Christmas and Happy Holidays to all, and to all a good night.

ल्ऋ

A TALE OF GOOD WILL

SOMETIMES, DECEMBER IS the hardest month in which to find Christmas.

It's there, all right, but it's under all the bows, lights, wreaths, ribbons, and gifts. Sometimes Christmas is a memory of something special, a memory that we bring out at this time of year and enjoy all over again.

This small tale is about a time that Christmas came in October on a rather ordinary street in Boston, and is for all the children who are already wise and kind, as well as for those who wish that they were a little more so.

A family of five people, made up of two parents, their two older sons, and their baby boy, made their way through the streets of Boston one afternoon, each in a foul humor. They had visited a museum and were trying to make their way through the crowded streets of that part of Boston known as the North End.

Many people strolling, cars turning suddenly, and some confusion as to the location of the restaurant they were trying to visit left each member of the family sniping at the others—the parents grumbled, the children pushed and pulled at one another—even the baby, perhaps the wisest of them all, looked into each face as if to say, *What has gone wrong with us today?*

As the decidedly unhappy group made its way along the cracked and meandering sidewalk, a man and woman several years older than the parents approached from the opposite direction. They walked stiffly, as if set apart from the rest of the people strolling, and somehow seemed quite alone—as if they had gotten used, a long time ago, to keeping tightly together.

As the two groups came closer, the family saw that the woman in the couple was very disfigured about the face, causing murmurs and glances from others as they passed.

Just as the two groups were preparing to pass one another, the man in the couple, who was jingling a handful of change, lost a penny from his bunch, and the old, rusty penny rolled into the gutter.

Quick as a wink, the middle child in the family left the others and went over to the gutter, plunging his hands into the dirty water, beginning to search for the lost penny. His baseball cap shielded most of his young face as he felt around among the cigarette butts, dented cans, and rotted paper for the coin.

The coin was not to be found easily, and his parents, their arguments forgotten, watched their son groping around in the dirty water and looked to each other, their eyes filling with tears. They didn't go to help their boy; it was his gift to give. He had moved beyond them suddenly, beyond all their teachings meant to demonstrate goodness and their words meant to impress charity.

The man who had lost the coin cleared his throat and watched the boy intently as people walked around the small group. The disfigured woman smiled a wonderful smile. The boy stood up, the lost penny clasped between his grimy fingers.

"Here you are," he said kindly, handing the man his penny back.

"You have quite a boy there," the man said to the parents, his voice maybe gruffer than usual, with perhaps a hint of a tear in it. They knew it; they had seen the young boy win many trophies, get many fine school reports, and yet they had never been prouder.

And so, on the streets of the North End of Boston, as people milled about and delivery trucks came and went, good will fell over a small part of the big city, and there was the feeling of Christmas. Everything you need to have a true Christmas was present: a gift given humbly, a thankful spirit, and a concern for how another is doing.

Even the wise and wondering baby was there, like the baby Jesus who was born in a manger and watched over by simple shepherds and gentle animals and who knew all about pennies.

Seasons greetings and merry Christmas, children.

May you have the chance to return a penny this holiday season—or have one returned to you.

ജ

BIRTHDAY GIRL

WELL, I'VE JUST celebrated another birthday. I happen to love my birthday, and I come from a long line of folks who take birthdays seriously, as well. I am not the type to say, "Well, at this age birthdays just aren't as big a deal as they once were." To the contrary, on the morning of my birthday I resemble Max, the dog from *The Grinch Who Stole Christmas*, when he thinks he's going to get to ride on the sleigh, and is not aware he's going to be pulling it instead. My ears are cocked, eyes bright, tongue wagging as I pant, "Presents? Cake? Charades? Bring them on!"

I don't get all caught up in the chronological age thing—which lets you know I'm getting up there. And I spend more time than I'd like to admit assessing my health as I age.

I was at Stop 'N' Shop the other day and actually found myself taking my own blood pressure at one of those free blood pressure stations. Before I knew it I was sitting in a hard plastic chair, my cart pulled up nearby, my baby boy in that cart, while a blood pressure cuff automatically started puffing up on my arm.

In truth, you feel kind of silly sitting there taking your own pressure—it's not like I have any kind of medical background. I was basically sitting low to the ground nodding sagely at shoppers going by in order to receive two numbers that would mean nothing to me.

By the posted guide on the machine my blood pressure was very good, and I had an obnoxious desire to brag about it.

Ten years ago I might have proudly said to a stranger in a shopping line, "You know, it's finally occurred to me that life is a stream, and we are its fishermen—in the most metaphorical of ways, that is. Cast your line, yeah, take a chance. Kind of a Crosby, Stills and Nash vibe, if you know what I mean."

Now I just wanted to get in that line and say, "120 over 70—hah!"

So, things are changing. But, I still love my birthday. The thing is, I live with a husband and three boys, so the finer nuances—you know, the cake, the presents, the cards—sometimes escape them. But when you're a good mom, you swallow your pride and do a little gentle reminding.

I spelled out my age in shaving cream on the mirror. I faked phone calls from friends, grinning into the dial tone and repeating, "You marvelous friend, you! You remembered! You're going to heaven!"

Pretending to be working on a crossword puzzle, I asked my boys as they walked by, "Say, what's a 13-letter phrase that rhymes with 'Sappy Perthbay'?"

Finally I spelled it out. "When you care about someone, it means a lot to that someone if you show it, so that they know how much they mean to you."

They looked at each other worriedly and said, "We've got to call Grandma right away."

Okay, I thought, on the morning of my birthday— there's still my husband. We've still got that ol' magic- –he'll be planning something good. And he didn't let me down.

"Right after I replace the car battery and take a look at that sluggish toilet, the night is yours, birthday girl!"

See what I mean?

You know what they say about the best-laid plans.

My birthday was the day our 15-month-old decided to enter the terrible twos.

As I was playing Solitaire on the computer (good moms take some time out to "just be") the baby walked by and shut off the whole computer without breaking stride.

Just as I was figuring that out, I heard gurgling. Tracking its source, I found the baby trying to encourage the cat to have a drink by drowning it in a cereal bowl full of milk he had pulled from the table.

"Ni ka-ka," (nice kitty) he murmured appreciatively, cutting off the cat's oxygen.

Then we proceeded to rid the neighbor's garden of some pesky old flowers, run down the street in our diaper while spewing a juice box all over ourselves, and poke out both Mommy's eyes with our fake plastic car keys. And that was just the morning.

I wasn't feeling very much like a birthday girl as I sealed off all exits to the roof and nailed furniture to the floor. I revised my plans—what are we, if not adaptable?

So maybe I was a little too worn out for dinner out, but we could still order in—and I would take this opportunity to curl up and watch *The Way We Were*, one of my favorite '70s movies.

When my husband came home I was still in my pajamas and sweat socks and smelled like a juice press.

"The baby is wearing me out," I moaned from my pillow. "I've got to watch *The Way We Were*."

Not quite understanding how these two ideas meshed but still trying hard to please, he handed me some cards and a present. I received a neat pair of running shoes, which is fortunate because that is apparently all I will be doing from now on.

And I had an ordinary birthday night, watching

The Way We Were. And I had some very strange dreams that night, where Barbra Streisand and Robert Redford whispered "Ni ka-ka" to each other!

ℛ

ELECTION DAY

A S AMERICANS, NOT long ago we found ourselves in an election year. Election year is a time when the public hears many speeches, is barraged with much information about the candidates involved, and has many of their favorite TV shows preempted for political debates and such.

I personally know it is a big election year when a two-term President does more fun activities as he is on his way out. I know that when I worked at the local sub shop in high school and had given my two-week notice, I was a lot more relaxed, so it works at all levels of American life.

There are basically three types of people when it comes to voting, and these people are categorized into groups by pollsters. (Pollsters are people who talk on the phone a lot and wear a lot of chinos.)

There is Polling Group #1, who are citizens who study up on candidates and issues and can talk intelligently about a "flat tax" or a "party platform," for example. These are the people who will make you feel really bad at a party. Just when you feel proud of yourself for leaving the house with all kids accounted for and having your panty hose on straight, this person will say in an earnest and friendly way, "So, Deirdre, how do you feel about the current Medicaid program?"

"My pantyhose are on straight," I stammer, going to stand by the punchbowl.

Then there are people who plain old don't know and don't care and will flat-out tell you that. This is Polling Group #2. I haven't fallen that far yet; I still like to pretend that I know what's going on.

I am in Polling Group #3. This group is of some concern to pollsters. We are the people who need the printed directions available at voting places that explain how to work the voting machine. We are the people who get a vague look on our faces when in a discussion about anything municipal that starts with the word "Proposition." We need a little more explanation than that.

We even sometimes, if we're really clueless, go by how the candidate's name sounds to us in the privacy of the voting booth; you have a much better chance of getting our vote if your name is John Itakecareayoo than you do if your name is John Smith.

Now, this is not to say I'm proud of this. I'm trying to change. I'm trying to get out there and gather information; last time, I called my dad up and asked him who I should vote for. So the effort is there.

The first televised debate of the last election was held in Boston, not far from where I live.

"I think we should have the kids stay up later than usual and watch the debate tonight," I said to my husband as he struggled to balance the checkbook at the kitchen table.

"Uh huh," he grunted, clearly as interested in democracy as I was. "Where are your receipts?"

Now, I expected a fight from my kids when I told them that we were all going to watch the debate, but I forgot one sure truth that you can depend on about kids: they will watch anything if it means staying up late. They will watch *NOVA*, they will watch commercials, they will watch old videos of their parents replacing tile grout in the downstairs bathroom. They just want to remain conscious as long as possible, until their parents' nerves are a jangled mess and those parents are speaking incoherently from the need to be alone for a few minutes.

"Let's snuggle up under the blankets and you can make some cookies," my 11-year-old said, turning the TV on, while my teen-ager, who doesn't want to hang out with us anymore, asked if he could watch the debate in Utah. Finally though, we were all assembled.

The debate started, and the tension was high. The candidates dove right in, tackling many complex issues.

"What do you think?" I asked my 11-year-old, who was studying the TV intently.

"The one on the left has a really straight nose," was his comment.

"His nose goes all the way up into his forehead," he continued, to which I replied, "Don't all our noses go right up into our foreheads?"

We then as a family proceeded to feel our own noses to see if they go right up into our foreheads, while the candidates droned on about welfare, education, and health care in the background.

By the end of the debate my husband was covertly reading *Sports Illustrated*, our 11-year-old was hanging upside-down off the couch petting the cat, our teen-ager had declared us pawns of the ruling class, and I was mentally re-wallpapering the hallway.

It's not that we don't care; we just have the attention span of fleas by the end of a long day. We're going to get more involved, though.

And there is one political term I understand—the one about being in power and yet being powerless; I am a parent, so I'm the quintessential Lame Duck.

CR

COSMIC BOWLING

HAVE YOU EVER gone beyond the limits of your own endurance? Have you ever tested yourself in ways you never could dream that you'd be tested? Have you ever taken ten kids "Cosmic Bowling" for a birthday party? I have. And I'm back to tell the tale.

My ten-year-old decided that for his eleventh birthday he would like to take 30 close pals bowling. I got him to whittle that list down to ten close pals, at which point he then let me know that he wanted to go "Cosmic Bowling." I had never heard of such a phenomenon but was assured by him that it was "wicked awesome" and "totally cool."

With recommendations like that, who could say no? First, I checked with my husband via a phone call to his work. "Would you be willing to drive ten screaming kids to a faraway town so that they can cosmic bowl?" I asked. "Okey-dokey," he replied, "sounds great." I sensed that he was a tad preoccupied, but hey, okey-dokey means okey-dokey.

The next step was to call the bowling alley to book the bowling party, which turned out to be a lot like booking a wedding reception what with all the different party options available.

"I just want to bring a few kids bowling!" I said into the phone, as I was offered a choice of Plans A, B, C, or D—the kids were actually offered a choice of chicken or fish. A champagne toast was optional. I scribbled the unexpected variety of packages down as I pondered whether to go with a polka band or something a little more traditional during the bowling.

The next step was to pick out some clever and creative party invitations and then forget them in my purse for two weeks. This necessitated some furious phone calling two days before the party. The moms I was calling were all friends of mine, so I was allowed to use Mommy Shorthand when speaking—"Hi, it's me. Messed up, left invitations in bag. Cosmic Bowling. Monday night. I'll drive. Are you in?"

Each conversation lasted eight seconds—I had a party together in one minute and 20 seconds.

Finally the big day arrived. My husband and I, along with one of my girlfriends, carted ten kids plus our 15-month-old baby down the highway caravan-style; at every light my husband pulled up next to me and, in the time-honored tradition of circling your index finger around your ear, let me know that his carload was acting crazy.

My truckload was very productive, I'd have to say— on the ride up we settled definitively which boy was oldest, who had swallowed a coin or marble in his lifetime, and who out of all of us had a roof big enough for a helicopter to land on.

We made it to the bowling alley in one piece, the boys all traded smelly shoes for smelly bowling shoes, and we were ready to go. Standing at the lanes suddenly the lights went out, disco balls dropped from the ceiling, and loud music started blaring. It was similar to an air raid in a World War II movie. When you're ten you call it "wicked cool," when you're in your thirties you call it "a seizure waiting to happen." My girlfriend handed me a Coke and some Tylenol without even asking.

I tried to be with it; I showed a few of the kids how to do the Macarena in the pulsing darkness—I looked like a mime stuck in a box.

The baby looked around in wonder at the strobe lights and disco balls and kept turning to stare at me as if to say, *Just when I think I have this planet all figured out . . .*

The kids were in their element, yet took a few moments out of the frenzied activities to share their thoughts and feelings with us. "Where's the food?" "I feel sick," and "Timmy is in the bathroom again," were just a few of those thoughts.

We were all having a ball, and, except for the time when some kid or other suggested that we use the baby to retrieve gutter balls, I'd say the party was a smash. In the party room, as kids laughed and ran around and paper straw wrappers whizzed through the air, I watched my son talk and laugh—still a little boy, soon not a little boy at all.

Next year is middle school, and he probably won't wear a blue ribbon won at Field Day pinned to his shirt all day, happily forgotten. We probably won't stumble upon him playing with his matchbox cars in a patch of sunlight as much as we do now. I probably won't feel his hand in mine nearly as often as I'd like.

It's his birthday, but we have received the gift. And this summer, if you ask my husband or me what age breaks your heart, we'll probably answer, "Ten, going on 11."

ΟΆ

MOTHER'S DAY

ONE OF MY favorite holidays is coming up—Mother's Day. This is the day when moms all over the country are pampered and appreciated for all they do for their family—unless of course, the dad of the family has a pre-existing golf date—if this should occur, mom can be feted sometime later.

Traditionally, on Mother's Day the mom is given gifts. My Mother's Day gifts always vary wildly according to the status of my husband's time and our bank account—one year I was given a new dress and a reservation at a fancy restaurant; another year I was given a twig in a clay pot.

Children's gifts, of course, are the most meaningful—I remember one year, when my kids were little, waking to the wonderful smell of toast covered with pennies, which of course was served with a tall glass of milk, juice, and coffee grounds all mixed together—nobody says my kids can't economize.

My favorite thing to do on Mother's Day, however, is to go out to breakfast. Apparently I am not alone in this—the last year we went out we joined the rest of the free world at the door to Denny's restaurant.

Now, no matter how many combined hours of my life I have spent standing on the sidewalk outside Denny's, I never learn—I will do anything to sit in a vinyl booth and devour a "Scram Slam" or a "Moons Over My Hammy" on Mother's Day.

My husband and kids may squirm and sigh, but hand me a big fat newspaper and promise me some coffee at some point, and I will wait forever.

The last time we went to Denny's for Mother's Day may be the last, I'm afraid. I don't know if my family can take it. It's just too crowded. Moms are everywhere, closing their eyes and willing their name to be called by the hostess—a name that they will probably not recognize because their husband lost his mind when giving a name to the hostess and gave the name William when everyone in the universe calls him Bill.

When you have not yet made it to the lobby but are still outside, all you can do is stand on the sidewalk holding your newspaper, that weighs fifty pounds and keeps falling apart, and stare through the glass at the people inside, commenting on how slow they are eating.

"Oh, look at that," my husband can be heard mumbling, "they don't need more coffee! Have you ever seen anything like it? They are sitting back and relaxing! Let's move it, people—they need to be doing more eating!"

My kids are pushing each other into the shrubs, and I am craning my neck to see how the line is progressing. Some people in line just give up and drop out, heading for their cars while saying, "This is ridiculous!" I give a sympathetic eye-roll, but hey, it means I'm that much closer to a choice of syrups and sugar in packets.

We make it into the lobby, and somehow this feels like a huge accomplishment, like we've just run a 10k race or something, instead of the somewhat measly accomplishment of following a bunch of strangers through a door.

The hard part about being inside is that you can smell the food, and sometimes you can see a glimpse of it go by. There is nowhere to sit, and those who are sitting will only move in the case of a fire—it would have to be a really big fire—or, of course, if their names are called by the hostess.

My kids immediately head for an amusement set up in the waiting area—a glass-encased game like one that you would find in an arcade. This particular game has the participant maneuvering a claw-like metal arm over a bunch of rumpled stuffed animals in an attempt to grab one of these "prizes," an attempt that is futile 100% of the time.

"Give us some quarters, Dad," the kids say, while my husband reaches into his pocket, then squints to examine his change in the dusky light of the hallway leading to the restrooms.

"I think those are quarters," he says.

A few minutes later, the whole waiting area is becoming engrossed in the game the boys are playing.

"I think he's got it," an elderly gentleman says excitedly to his wife, peering through his glasses at my son's maneuvering. His wife, having lapsed into what professional doctors call "The Denny's Coma," mumbles, "No one is ever going to win," and falls asleep again.

Finally, our names are called. Giggling happily, we approach our table like it was an old and dear friend. "Well now," we say, sliding into the booth, "this looks perfect!" All of us, children and adults, immediately start working on the coloring projects on our menus, just to give our brains some time to expand back into our heads.

I look around contentedly. Here I am, surrounded by my family. Sure, the kids are exhausted, dehydrated and cranky, fighting with each other like wildcats. And, okay, my husband is gluing placemats together with his own spit in order to flag down some coffee. But the point is, soon I will be eating a "Scram

Slam" while surrounded by my family.

So, maybe we weren't exactly happy, but we were together. A good mom never asks for more than that.

CR

D EIRDRE REILLY is a freelance humor columnist whose column appears in many Community Newspaper Company, Inc., publications throughout Massachusetts. Her work has also appeared in *The Hartford Courant* and *Boston Herald* newspapers and the literary journal, *Cimarron Review*. Deirdre lives outside Boston, Massachusetts, with her husband and three boys.

ଔ   ଔ

Direct Order Form

EXHAUSTED RAPUNZEL
Tales of Modern Castle Life
—Deirdre Reilly

Mail this order (pay by check, credit card or money order) to:
Opine Publishing - P.O. Box 1239 - Columbia, MD 21044
(Credit Card phone orders: 443-745-1004)
Number of Books:
_____@ $13.00 each .... $_____
(12% off $14.95 regular price)
[**Sales Tax:** Please add 5% for Maryland orders] .. $_____
Shipping & Handling, U.S.:
*Add $3.95 per book... $_____
          TOTAL .... $_____

Method of Payment:
❑ US Money Order, enclosed, M.O. # _____
❑ Check, enclosed, check # _____
❑ Credit card: ___Visa ___MasterCard
   Card #_____Exp. Date:_____
   Name on Card_____
   Card Billing Address:

   _____

   _____

   Signature _____

Ship to Address:

NAME:_____

ADDRESS:_____

CITY:_____STATE_____ZIP_____

E-mail (optional): _____Telephone_____

*To inquire about Special Bulk Order Shipping Rates (3 or more books), inquire by phone: 443-745-1004, fax: 410-730-0917 or e-mail: info@opinepublishing.com

Opine Publishing

Direct Order Form

EXHAUSTED RAPUNZEL
Tales of Modern Castle Life
—Deirdre Reilly

Mail this order (pay by check, credit card or money order) to:
Opine Publishing - P.O. Box 1239 - Columbia, MD 21044
(Credit Card phone orders: 443-745-1004)

Number of Books:

____@ $13.00 each .... $_____
(12% off $14.95 regular price)
[**Sales Tax:** Please add 5% for Maryland orders] .. $_____
Shipping & Handling, U.S.:
*Add $3.95 per book.. $_____

TOTAL .... $_____

Method of Payment:

❑ US Money Order, enclosed, M.O. # _____

❑ Check, enclosed, check # _____

❑ Credit card: ___Visa ___MasterCard
Card #_____Exp. Date:_____
Name on Card_____
Card Billing Address:

_____

_____

Signature _____

Ship to Address:

NAME:_____

ADDRESS:_____

CITY:_____STATE_____ZIP_____

E-mail (optional): _____Telephone_____

*To inquire about Special Bulk Order Shipping Rates (3 or more books), inquire by phone: 443-745-1004, fax: 410-730-0917 or e-mail: info@opinepublishing.com

Opine Publishing

Direct Order Form

EXHAUSTED RAPUNZEL
Tales of Modern Castle Life
—Deirdre Reilly

Mail this order (pay by check, credit card or money order) to:
Opine Publishing - P.O. Box 1239 - Columbia, MD 21044
(Credit Card phone orders: 443-745-1004)

Number of Books:

_____@ $13.00 each .... $_____
      (12% off $14.95 regular price)
[**Sales Tax:** Please add 5% for Maryland orders] .. $_____
Shipping & Handling, U.S.:
*Add $3.95 per book .... $_____

              TOTAL .... $_____

Method of Payment:

❑ US Money Order, enclosed, M.O. # _____

❑ Check, enclosed, check # _____

❑ Credit card: ___Visa ___MasterCard
    Card #_____Exp. Date:_____
    Name on Card_____
    Card Billing Address:
    _____
    _____
    Signature _____

Ship to Address:

NAME:_____

ADDRESS:_____

CITY:_____STATE_____ZIP_____

E-mail(optional): _____Telephone_____

*To inquire about Special Bulk Order Shipping Rates (3 or more books), inquire by phone: 443-745-1004, fax: 410-730-0917 or e-mail: info@opinepublishing.com

Printed in the United States
894800002B